Personal Revelations
of
Our Lady of Light

Introduction, Commentary and
General Editing *by*

Gerald G. Ross

.

Dedication

To the Marian Movement of Priests
and to those who serve it's cause
and to
God the Father's Ministers
of all walks of Faith

PEACE BE WITH YOU

In conformity with the decrees by Pope Urbanus VIII, the Publisher recognizes and accepts that the final authority regarding the messages of Our Lady of Light rests with the Holy See of Rome, to whose judgment we willingly submit.

*The decree of the Congregation for Propagation of the Faith A.A.S. 58, 1186 (approved by Pope Paul VI on October 14, 1966) states that the Imprimatur is no longer required on publications that deal with new revelations, apparitions, prophesies or miracles, provided that they contain nothing contrary to faith and morals.
—The Publisher

Published by Our Lady of Light Publications.

For additional copies, write to:
Our Lady of Light Publications
P.O. Box 17541
Fort Mitchell, KY 41017

Copyright © 1992 Gerald G. Ross

Library of Congress Catalog Card No.: 92-093603

ISBN: 0-9635852-0-7

St. Joseph Church, Cold Spring, Kentucky

St. Joseph statue in church bell tower

Table of Contents

Appreciation

My thanks to those who gave their encouragement and talents whether counsel, or typing, or editing, or proofreading, or legal, or photography. I extend my appreciation for the sincerity of their assistance. To the anonymous visionary and to the locutionist goes my deep appreciation for their special help. To my lovely wife for her support and sincere interest, I extend my love and heartfelt thanks.

St. Joseph parking area where 6 to 8000 gathered in August 31

St. Joseph rectory and parking area to left

Gratitude

For the guidance that her messages be considered as "requests" and be spread as "personal revelations" as they are personal to all that she touches; to keep it simple as her ways are always as such; that it would please her if a picture was prominent, showing her to the left of the Crucifix, as her messages everywhere are to bring her children to Jesus and back to God—for this dear lady your apprentice is most grateful.

Fr. Smith is moderator at the Sunday Marian
Movement of Priests Lay Cenacle

Chapter I

Introductory Comments

1. A Reflection

Looking back one can see the grace of God in the gradual evolvement of events. It all started with the touching of the heart of a priest, Fr. Leroy Smith, then pastor at St. Theresa Catholic Church in Southgate, a Kentucky suburb of Greater Cincinnati. Following his trip to Medjugorje in October 1988, he formed a prayer group at his parish. Soon his prayer groups started attracting people from all of the nearby tri-state communities.

As you read through the essence of this book, the experience, the claimed ''requests'' and the messages from Our Lady and Jesus, Fr. Smith is central to all of its activities and people.

It is not intended here to establish creditability of these alleged visions and messages. What is intended is to publish all that is considered pertinent, even to the extent of including what rightly might be considered insignificant. Issues of creditability and theology are for future qualified authorities. Some of these issues and statements may be considered startling and draw comments from church leaders. Readers are thus cautioned to understand individual statements in terms of total context.

The material presented has been grouped so that the visionary's personal experiences are separate from Our Lady's

1

requests and messages from Jesus. We have maintained the date sequencing of the messages.

The locutionist's letters and experiences are also segregated in a separate chapter and presented by date.

In order to protect the anonymity of the visionary, all personal names, with the exception of the Arkansas locutionist, have been deleted from "Her Personal Experiences."

This story begins with a letter being written on December 8, 1991, allegedly a dictation by a lady who identified herself as the Queen of Peace and the Mother of God, to a reputed locutionist, Mrs. Cyndi Cain of Bella Vista, Arkansas. This was personal correspondence; an excerpt of portions of this letter, which appear in Chapter VII, foretold that St. Joseph's would be a place of great devotion, a place where immeasurable graces were to pour forth, a place where Our Lady would manifest herself and a place where there would occur healings and conversions. Appropriate advice was solicited by Fr. Smith, and he was counseled to proceed prudently and to await further direction from Our Lady.

On Mother's Day, May 10, 1992, at the Notre Dame Marian Conference, a woman from a neighboring suburb of Ohio, who was experiencing apparitions and messages from Our Lady, was advised by Our Lady to contact Fr. Leroy Smith at St. Joseph Church in Cold Spring, Kentucky. She had heard of Fr. Smith but did not know him personally. Following a brief period of doubt and fear, she contacted Fr. Smith, and the events and this story began to unfold.

The method chosen to tell this story is the medium of the messages. Our Lady refers to them specifically as her "requests."

2. What is the Phenomenon?

What we are concerned with here are charisms, which include private revelations and apparitions. Charisms are extraordinary powers given a Christian by the Holy Spirit for the good of the Church, for the upbuilding of the body of Christ. They are a phenomena that have often occurred in the life of the Church. There seems to be an outpouring of charisms at the present time. Our Lady of Light mentions this thusly:

"I am appearing to many at this time and in many different places. As to the creditability of my messages being sent through many of my messengers, they will prove their own accuracy—as many shall bring forth the fruit of faith—and the unfoldment *of my messages will be the proof."*

The words of St. Thomas Aquinas come to mind: "The purpose of private revelations is not to prove the truths of Christian Doctrine or to add anything to it. It is given to men of a certain period, because of the circumstances of that period direction."

The messages of Our Lady stress the urgency of her requests. Every aspect of society seems to be turning away from God at an accelerating rate. It seems as if her urgency corresponds to the timing of our needs. Do her messages fit our requirements?

What about mistakes, errors, misinterpretations and slanting toward one's own will? Can this phenomenon, these charisms, even if judged creditable, be subject to these kinds of happenings? Of course it can. Our Lady and her Son use the medium of the human free will. That is partially why the final creditability issue rests in the fruits of and/or the judgment by proper and qualified authorities. All messages here are to be considered alleged.

In the matter of private or personal revelations, the human element is always involved. God or Our Lady speaks to the individual in a manner consistent with that person's understanding. The messenger will then be able to explain, in their own human terms, what has been revealed.

You might also apply Our Lady's words, *"Look beyond what your physical eyes are beholding, and you will see a greater plan at work."* In other words try to determine the real issues, look at them constructively, and decide wisely. Discerning is a topical term now in view of all that has transpired. Try to keep from being judgemental under the guise of prayerful discernment.

3. Why This Book?

The decision to publish these messages was made in mid-August, prior to the August 31 foretold date. It was made with a complete sense of confidence, the logic resting in the often quoted guidance of His Holiness, Pope Urban VIII (1623-1644).

> "In cases which concern private revelations, it is better to believe than not to believe, for if you believe, and it is proven true, you will be happy that you have believed, because your Holy Mother asked it. If you believe, and it should be proven false, you will receive all blessings as if it had been true, because you believed it to be true."

Although the proof lies in the fruits, I have always felt a balanced application of this guidance to be crucial to any such discernment.

There is, of course, the greater reason: the deep, longing hope that all of this is real—that God the Father has chosen to so highly honor all of His earthly children here in this area of our country and in this church of St. Joseph in this small Kentucky community with the unique and fitting name of Cold Spring. It stills the mind just to imagine that God would send our Blessed Mother, His single perfection of humanity, the one foretold who is to conquer the essence of evil for all time, to be here with us as part of this great process. Can this be truly real? The messages say emphatically, "yes." If it be so, it is hoped our sense of community spirituality responds and receives her with great veneration and humility.

There are other reasons for publishing and for doing so quickly. One is an alleged **urgent** request of Our Lady to do so. Secondly, there are issues raised in the messages of Our Lord and His Mother that seem startlingly new, novel and important. They will be discussed in the commentary chapter and in the editor's notes associated with some of the messages.

4. St. Joseph Church

St. Joseph Catholic Church in Cold Spring, Kentucky, is located on the left going south on Alexandria Pike, U.S. 27, which is just outside the greater Cincinnati circle free-way, I-275. It's about seven miles from downtown Cincinnati. St. Joseph is a rather large church with a capacity of over a thousand, and serves other communities as well as Cold Spring. The present church property dedicated in 1960, comprises 22 acres. On it are also located a convent, a large grade school with gym and new auditorium, an old school building now used for differing purposes, three spacious paved parking areas, a large rectory which adjoins the church and a quite large open sports field at the rear of the property. Ongoing activities bring a steady stream of people.

5. Fr. R. Leroy Smith, Pastor, St. Joseph Church

Fr. Leroy Smith was ordained June 5, 1954. His priesthood started as secretary to Bishop Mulloy, then grew to include twelve years as Vice Rector and teacher at St. Pius X Seminary and eventually involved three pastorates; St. Joseph in Cresent Springs, St. Theresa in Southgate, and, since July 1991, St. Joseph in Cold Spring, Kentucky. His first trip to Medjugorje in October 1988 was a turning point in his life. In his own words, "My spiritual life has deepened dramatically. I have always had a great devotion to Our Lady, but that has increased a hundredfold."

When he transferred to St. Joseph Church, his prayer groups came also: his weekly Friday night "core" group (those who had accompanied him on one of his early trips to Medjugorje), and his third Monday of each month Medjugorje prayer group, which draws an attendance of several hundred people from the tri-state area.

The Monday night Medjugorje group begins with several priests hearing confessions, followed by a Rosary, the Chaplet of Divine Mercy, and Mass (with homily). Everyone then moves over to Memorial Hall for a discussion of a spiritual subject and a brief social period.

Fr. Smith also has an area Mother of God Marian Movement of Priests laity cenacle which meets on the first Sunday of each month, and, lastly, the Our Lady of Light monthly priest cenacle which meets on the second Thursday of each month.

Fr. Smith is an eloquent speaker with fine tonal quality in his voice. Preaching is the gift Our Lady has developed in his mind and his heart. He never prepares a talk. The Holy Spirit and Our Lady seem to equip him spontaneously in Their own special way. An important homily is no apparent effort. His words always seem to fit the occasion. This devotion also shows in different ways—sometimes just a brief timely discourse or leading a song after Mass. He's traditional in his ways and his thoughts, and has a great sense of loyalty to the Pope, the Magisterium and with the Tradition of the Church.

He has two sisters and a brother, but his family is much larger than that. For him it also includes the close members of his prayer groups, his parish and those friends and interests he has built up over the years. Father Smith enjoys people, especially the company of those whose common interests and experiences tie them together. Their interchange flows quickly and spontaneously and his is always tactful. His friends seem to fill his life, and he theirs. He loves his parish priesthood and is totally dedicated to it. Most all of his thoughts and concerns center around his mission in life. The Church, his parish and his prayer groups are very serious parts of his overall sense of responsibility.

What's his outstanding characteristic? It's his great ability to love and he expresses that in leadership—in speaking and spreading the word of God and moving forward the messages of Our Holy Mother in everything he touches. It matters not whether it is a Marian Conference, a counseling session, a homily, a pilgrimage, a prayer group, a priestly cenacle, a seminary renovation, speaking for Our Lady at non-Catholic churches and rest homes, a Medjugorje anniversary, or a gathering at a friend's home. His leadership comes forth in everything where he's asked. Wherever or however Our Lady or her Son beckon, he goes, he does, he leads.

Our Lady said she had chosen him for this special mission because of his love and devotion, and that she would walk with him to the Father. Those who know Fr. Smith feel that's true.

6. The Church of the Steps

One may ask, "Is there another church involved?" Yes, in a sense. It is the Church of the Immaculata located on the pinacle of Mt. Adams in Cincinnati where it overlooks the Ohio River and the geographic area. It has been the site of the annual Good Friday Pilgrimage where, since 1860, the devout have climbed the steps leading up the church while praying the Rosary. The photo section gives the reader a good sense of this beautiful church named for Our Lady.

There are many reasons why Our Lady has allegedly chosen to grace this area with her presence, but undoubtedly one reason is the prayers said on these steps. One of her messages contains the following statement: *"The faithful souls that walked the way of the cross with my Son to my church on the hill has found favor with the Father, and my visit to your area is a special grace bestowed on you at this time."*

Although the Good Friday Rosary observance has been a custom for over 130 years, countless Rosary prayers have been answered at all times of the year. The high overlook provides a picturesque panorama of the geographic area. The inside of Immaculata Church is spiritually charming with its beautiful paintings and the two shrines of Our Lady of Lourdes and Our Lady of Fatima.

You will note the following statement in message number six of the Hidden Flower. *"It is my wish that the 'witness of my signs'—to her—be used as testimony to the fact of my real presence at the church named in honor of my spouse—as well as my church on the hill."*

Chapter II

The Visionary's Personal Experiences

A Dream

January 31, 1990, I had a strange but very comforting dream.

I dreamed I was in a huge church of some kind; it seemed like a "museum" with a chapel or small church inside it. I was with a crowd of people looking at a statue of "The Pieta."

While I was looking at the Holy Mother's face on the statue, it suddenly came to life, the head and face only. I was a little frightened and started telling the other people around me, "Look, look at her face. Do you see her? She's alive."

Then her eyes opened. She raised her head and looked at me. There was much intense suffering and longing in her face. She didn't say anything. I just felt some of her agony and pain as she looked down at her crucified Son that she was holding in her arms.

I was very excited then and wanted everyone to see what I was seeing, but no one else seemed to be aware of it.

I left the group and started looking in other rooms. It seems like I was searching for my children. I wanted to tell them and wanted them to see what I was seeing. I was also impatient because the other people I told seemed bored or not concerned with what I was trying to tell them. I felt others were appearing to agree with me, but only in order to pacify me. I rounded up my children and returned to the large room, but when we got there, the statue was gone. There was only the empty pedestal.

I left the crowded room and started looking in other rooms down the long hallways of this large place.

Finally, after searching in vain for the missing statue, I returned to the room where the statue had been.

Then I saw Jesus. On the pedestal where the statue of Mary had been, Jesus was standing. He was glowing brilliantly, and He was very large. He reached the high ceiling, and the light from Him filled the whole room.

At this point, I was jubilant, and the happiness that filled me cannot be described. I yelled out to everyone in the crowd, but they seemed not to notice at all. They paid no attention to me or to Jesus in their midst.

Jesus was smiling, and His eyes were sparkling. He reached His hands out for me, and I placed both my hands in His and felt such happiness I thought I would burst. I heard Him say, more in my thoughts than in actual words, *"I am always with you!"* Then, in what seemed to be actual words, I heard Him say, *"You will remember this. This is no dream."*

A special note here: Even after I seemed to wake up, I could still see Him, and He lit up my whole bedroom. At this point, I was directed (in my thoughts) to write all this down, which I did.

2. The Visionary's Personal Experiences   SEPT. 1, 1991

First Visit of "Our Lady of Light"

On Sunday evening, September 1, 1991, I was visiting a friend's farm in Indiana. My daughter, her friend, two other women and I went out into the field where we had built a campfire and were sitting around talking.

As night fell, we pulled our jackets around us and huddled closer to the campfire. Suddenly, we noticed a light coming from an area of trees several hundred yards away. On looking closer, it had the shape of a lady turned sideways.

As we all watched (for we all five saw her) she started

to turn toward us. Her hands were sometimes outstretched, and sometimes they were holding something.

I said out loud, "If you're not from the Lord, you're not welcome here." I then mentally heard, *"I am from the Lord. Because you honored my Son, I have come to you."*

One lady and I immediately fell to our knees and started praying our rosaries, which we had in our pockets. I asked (mentally) who she was, and I got this reply: *"I am the Lady of Light. Take my light and spread it into the darkness of ignorance overshadowing the earth."*

As we prayed, the lady got brighter and the surrounding trees appeared to be made of light. The area behind these trees would light up and then grow dimmer.

Again, I mentally asked what this light was, and she answered, *"It is the grace of God."*

She kept turning in different directions and at times would be holding the baby Jesus in front of her with His arms outstretched. At one time, she was holding a cross in front of her.

She continued to stay there, and I felt a feeling of peace pouring out from her to all of us. But I also felt an urgent silent pleading.

She said she was appearing to us as mothers because she needed all the mothers of American to reach the childen. There were other personal messages which she gave to each of us (mentally). She appeared a slight distance away from us and was in the branches of the trees.

At one point, there appeared to be three children in front of her. (Fatima?) Also, while we were praying the Rosary, one lady's rosary started glowing. (I would like to mention here that the lady whose farm we were visiting had been making rosaries and giving them away for a long time.)

Our Lady said she would appear to us again, and then she left.

This beautiful "light" appeared from about 9:30 p.m. until around midnight.

OCT. 19, 1991

The lady who owned the farm was with me again at a gathering at another location. We walked to view the land, as she had never been there before. When we started back through the field, we saw the same golden light as before and discovered that Our Lady had returned to us. Once again, she appeared as a figure of light in the trees.

3. The Visionary's Personal Experiences   OCT. 26-27, 1991

Chicago Marian Conference

My daughter and I accompanied my two aunts to the Chicago Marian Conference, October 26 and 27, 1991. Because one of my aunts has a hearing problem, we were placed in the front row near the speaker's stage.

While sitting there in front of the beautiful statue of Mary and the huge banner that reached to the ceiling with her countenance on it, and gazing at the very holy picture of Our Lady of Guadalupe, I struck up a conversation (in my mind) with Mary, Our Holy Mother, and she answered me (mentally).

She kept telling me to *"Purify your heart."* So, I kept praying and asking for forgiveness for all indiscretions and sins that I had committed—but she still only answered, *"Purify your heart."*

Later in the program, it was announced that confessions were being heard in the upper balconies, so I decided to go. My daughter said that she would go with me, as she too wanted to go to confession.

This truly was Our Lady at work, for my daughter had not been going to Church or the Sacraments for a very long time.

I was pleased and started praying to Our Lady (while we waited in line) to send her to the "right" priest so that he would be "kind" to her.

When we got to the front of the line, two priests were available at the same time. (There were six priests there hearing confessions.) So, I started for the one directly in front of me when I felt a tug on my elbow. I thought it was an usher, but when I looked, no one was there. Anyway, I was directed by this "invisible" tug to a priest at the far end of the hallway—sort of isolated—and my daughter went to the one I started to go to.

At the time I assumed that Our Lady had chosen that priest for her since I had asked for this favor from her. However, it was the other way around. She sent *me* to a "special" priest, one she presumably had hand-picked—as you will see from what transpires.

Needless to say, I had no intention of telling anyone about the apparitions I had been seeing. (I had only told a few close family members and friends.) And now I found myself "sharing" this experience with this priest. I told him that Our Lady wanted everyone to know that she is here and to tell them she has not forgotten the United States of America. I also told him that she was approaching the **Mothers of America** for she needed them to help her do her work here.

After this brief expulsion of a confidence, which I had intended to keep quiet, I wondered what had happened to me and why in the world I did that.

Well, now I know—I didn't. Our Lady did it. It was part of her plan. I'm still not sure just what all of her plan is and just where I fit in, but I'm sure she'll let me know. I'm also sure that this special "priest" of hers is a big part of her plan.

And now I want to explain (the best I can) what happened to me on that glorious day, October 26, 1991.

When I returned to my seat, the other three in my group had gone off to purchase something to eat. I found this time to be a good chance to talk and pray with Our Lady. Then I heard her say to me (mentally), *"Now your heart is pure."*

Then while sitting there gazing at the large picture of her on the curtains behind the stage, I noticed a rainbow had formed about her head, and the picture was glowing in the same golden light that she appeared in previously. And then I simply went into shock because the picture became the **real** lady. She was real as you and me. She was looking in the balconies and then slowly looking down at all the people with a big smile on her face.

She had no veil on, and her hair was full and flowing long. It was black, and it was parted slightly off-center. She had on a blue robe, and the dress under it was a paler blue. I could see her eyes clearly—especially when she looked down at me—right there in the front row.

She spoke to me (in my mind) and said many things.

First, she said, *"Yes, I am real. Tell the people I'm real. And so is the evil one, but I will not show you this now."*

Then she just looked around at everyone with a loving

smile. She was bathed in a golden light—much like sunshine—and was shimmering and glowing.

When people came up to the stage to pray to her, she would look down at them and smile. She also blessed the people praying in front of the picture of Our Lady of Guadalupe.

At me, she would mentally communicate messages as if we were having a normal conversation.

When my daughter came back and sat beside me, I whispered to her about what was happening and kept whispering to her things Our Lady was telling me. My daughter saw her for only an instant, and only her hair and not her face. However, she said she could see the golden light around her.

Our Lady said she needs the mothers of America and wants me to help her reach them. I stammered and stuttered that I wasn't worthy of any of this and asked why she had chosen me. I told her that I don't know how to do any of the things she was asking me.

She said that I was to tell a priest about this—and only one priest. Of course, I said, "I can't do that, dear Mother. I won't know who, or what to say. You know that if I start telling someone—even a priest—that I saw Our Lady, they'll say I'm either crazy or some kind of kook or something."

I continued to silently plead with her, "Can't we just keep all of this to ourselves?"

She just kept smiling and answered me, *"I'll send the priest to you tomorrow. You will not have to find one, for he will come to you. I will send him."*

Well, I still kept hedging and squirming about what she was asking me to do. "Dear Mother, I just can't do that. You understand, don't you?" Her only answer was her loving smile.

She kept looking around the crowd, smiling. She was telling them that she needed them as much as they needed her—especially pleading to the mothers there in the crowd. Her pleas were silent—but I heard them.

She said the children of America were spoiled and were selfish and their faith was lacking. She has come to America to rally the mothers and to help them save their children. She wants the mothers to change their lives into holy ones. She wants them to lead their children to her, and she will protect them under her mantle of motherly love.

She wants the mothers of America to **change** America—to lead every member of her family back to God. She said she can't do it alone without their help. She is willing if they are.

They must choose this, however, and ask for her help. Otherwise, she can do nothing. She wants the mothers here to be examples to all in their families. She is asking and waiting for our response.

She wants to remind us that the time grows short. She had to come to the people of America by calling the faithful ones to other holy spots first so that they could bring the peace they found there home with them.

The people in America have strayed so far from their God that this was the only way to reach them and awaken their spirits.

There was much more that I choose not to go into at this time.

When the speaker from the Ukraine, Josyp Terelya, came on stage, Our Lady looked at him with a great tenderness. I noticed that the same golden glow on her also surrounded him. She told me this was her protective mantle.

When a priest came on stage to bless this man, a golden light flowed from Our Lady's heart and covered them both, and the golden light seemed to pass from the priest into the man before him. Priests and all clergy should remember that whenever they give a blessing, Our Lady and her Son, Jesus, send their love to them to give to whomever they are blessing. A blessing is for real. I saw it.

Our Lady is also very real and she wants me to tell all of her people that she is. Especially the non-Catholics, for they are misinformed about her; she wants to meet them, for they are her "missing children," and she has much love to give them. As their mother, she can help them come closer to her Son. She said to tell them that we Catholics do not worship her. We worship only God and Jesus, her Son.

Also, she wanted it stressed that we do not pray **to** her in the sense of adoration, but to and WITH her as an intercessor. She is our intercession to Jesus and not His equal. She can cure no one, and she can perform NO miracles. She can only **ask** for it. She said that only God is the one who does the healing and grants graces which we call "miracles."

She does, however, have a powerful influence with her Son and can help us if only we will come to her and **ask**.

She said that all of the clergy, who are acting as God's apostles here, are like *windows* into God, showing the people who and what God is. She, however, is a *door* and can open a heart so that the soul can enter into the presence of God. She wants **all** of her children to know her and use her as the door she was meant to be.

It is our responsibility—the ones who have the truth—to share it and not keep it to ourselves. (I guess that's why I feel compelled to share this experience.)

Anyway, I was in the real and personal presence of the Blessed Virgin Mary on this night. She was there for a long time. I'm not too sure just how long it was, as time seemed to "stand still."

Our Lady gave me some personal messages, and then after smiling at the singers or speakers on stage, she just left, and the picture was simply a picture again.

Before I go on, however, there is one personal message I feel I should share. Our Lady told me that my mother, father and two brothers were there with her and that she could also tell me that my cousin, who had passed on just a short time ago, was indeed there and that she was with Jesus.

And then she said something that at first I didn't understand. She said she also had four of my grandchildren with her and that she would keep them there for me in her care. I was puzzled and wondered why she would say this because there had been no deaths of grandchildren in my family. And then it hit me—the miscarriages. Of course, that's it. Sadly, there had been four miscarriages between my children at early stages of their pregnancies.

It is such a comforting thought and a wonderful thing to know, not only for me, but also for any mothers who have lost any child, in any way. Our Blessed Mother has them. She calls them her angels, as are the children that are murdered by angry souls. Our Lady is also sending a powerful blessing to all the mothers of aborted children. It is *"for their salvation,"* she says. These mothers should know that Our Holy Mother said that there is **no** error that is not forgiven by her Son, Jesus. All they need to do is ask. He will send them peace if they will surrender their wills to Him.

Also, she said we should pray more to the Holy Spirit so that the ignorance of the spiritual life which is filling us can be replaced with knowledge and wisdom. She has come to help us convert and reconcile with our God, our Creator.

So, please, whoever you are reading this, whatever your walk in life, **listen** to her. She is speaking to you in the stillness of your soul. And then, do as she tells you. It is for your own good. And another thing, it is no coincidence if you find yourself reading this. For the Blessed Mother is calling **you!** And you are part of her plan.

And now, back to Sunday, October 27, 1991, the last day of the Marian Conference in Chicago.

We left our hotel early for the conference since we had to load our baggage on the bus for our return trip that afternoon. We were scheduled to leave immediately following the end of the program.

I had considered finding a priest and telling him about yesterday's experience but quickly dismissed it from my mind. I told Our Lady after I got home I would find a priest close to home and convey her wishes to him.

Well, let me tell you, Our Lady had other plans and apparently didn't hear any of my weak excuses.

For, lo and behold, just as she said, she produced her priest—right on schedule and just as she had planned all along. And guess who it was? Of course—the priest I had been to confession to the day before.

This is how it happened. That afternoon, two of our party had already boarded the bus, and I waited behind with my aunt for the conclusion of the ceremonies. As we were leaving, we decided to weave our way through the seats instead of battling the crowded corridors.

Just as we reached the door by which we were to leave, this priest came running up the steps and grabbed my hands.

"There you are," he stated. "I've been looking for you. I wanted to talk to you some more. I even sent my guardian angel to look for you, and he found you."

Let me tell you, you could have knocked me over with a feather. I looked at him and smiled at the picture of Mary on the curtain behind the stage (the one that became real), and replied, "No, your guardian angel didn't do it, she did it," as I pointed to Our Lady's picture, and I could have sworn that I almost saw her smile again.

Reluctantly, I agreed to share my experience with him, and took his card, which he graciously offered, promising to get in touch with him after I returned home. In turn, I gave him my address on the condition that I remain anonymous, because I didn't want to draw any attention to myself.

I have to be honest and say that I really had no intention at that time of offering this story to the public, and since my return home, I have been struggling and wrestling with the notion of just forgetting to write the priest and only tell my close family and friends.

However, Our Lady immediately admonished me for selfish behavior. She told me, *"I am everyone's Mother, and my messages here are for all, not just for you."* Well, I half-heartedly agreed to her desires, but I didn't say when.

I guess Jesus saw in my heart, because the next message I got (and even wrote) was from Him.

> *"If you wish to honor Me, do as My mother tells you! In ignoring her and her wishes, you also ignore Me. Why can't you remember that I am always with you? Focus on Me and we shall do it together!"*

That was pretty clear to me; so here I am, sharing.

I'd like to add here that I'm not trying to prove **anything** to **anybody**. I'm simply recording this for my own personal remembrance (and because Our Lady wished it).

I know it really happened just as related here. I believe! But it's up to each individual reading this material to determine that for themselves, and they have the choice to accept or reject, just as with all choices presented in life.

4. The Visionary's Personal Experiences   NOV. 18, 1991

A Miracle for December 8, 1991

While at the Chicago Conference, I received a message which I was to tell the priest that I had met there. I wrote it down after I returned home but did not do so until November 18, 1991, and I did so only after I was reminded by Our Lady to write it down for documentation. She reminded me that I did not tell the priest (from Maryland) about it yet.

So, I finally called him on the phone and told him. The message was this: Our Lady has promised a miracle for December 8, 1991.

I had no idea what she meant by "a miracle." I told him that perhaps he should look up in the sky for something to happen.

I also told several of my family members and close friends of her promise of an upcoming miracle.

5. The Visionary's Personal Experiences   NOV. 16, 1991

Another Visit of "Our Lady of Light"

On Saturday, November 16, 1991, while spending a weekend at my daughter's house, I had a great experience.

Not only did I see Our Lady (as a figure of light again) in the wooded area by the house, but was able to share it with many others, including some of my grandchildren.

A group of us went out for a walk in the field, and upon starting back, we all saw Our Lady.

We started praying the Rosary and again noticed that she would get brighter as we prayed. There were angels, as figures of light, with her. They appeared to be kneeling around her. For a short time, there was another figure of light beside her, and they appeared to be holding hands. Our Lady said she had brought my mother with her. My mother had spent the last ten years of her life in a nursing home and had passed away in May 1987. All of her life, however, she was very devoted to Our Lady and to Jesus.

Our Lady continued, *"Your mother is here with me and my Son. Much grace is bestowed on you family through her intercession."* Then she added, *"She will be permitted to remain with you a short while."*

There was another aspect that entered into this visit. Of course, being a doubter and still somewhat dazed by all this, whenever I am contacted by any spirit or spirits that I see or hear, I always say, "If you are not of the Lord, you are not welcome, and in the name of Jesus, you must leave." Needless to say, Our Lady always stays and seems pleased.

While Our Lady was visible to my daughter and I (the others being in the woods), a huge, dark form, as tall as a tree, seemed to appear a short distance away. We both noticed it and felt oddly uncomfortable about it. I immediately started praying the prayer to St. Michael, and I repeated, "If you are not of the Lord, you are not welcome."

Then Our Lady said, *"Wherever I am, the evil one is also. Pray that you do not fall under his influence. I shall help you to pray."*

Then a strange thing happened. A light from where she was seemed to shoot across to where the dark form was and seemed to encircle it, and then the dark form seemed to be erased by this light. Then, when the others emerged from the woods, they were not only talking about the light they saw by my daughter and I, but one of my grandchildren was excited about the mysterious light she saw dance across the ground. She had witnessed it also.

I have to add that I felt no fear about this dark form, only uncomfortable.

After the five of us went back into the house, we told some of the others what had happened, as there was a crowd of my family and friends there. Then my friend and I took some others of my grandchildren out to where Our Lady had been, and she showed herself to them, too. We prayed the rosary and watched her. When the light faded, we returned to the house.

6. The Visionary's Personal Experiences   **DEC. 8, 1991**

The Day of the Predicted Miracle

All day I was expecting the "miracle" that Our Lady had promised to send. I periodically looked up at the sky, expecting some paranormal event.

Near 6:00 p.m. I started praying to Our Lady and asking her about "her miracle" and if I was to go somewhere or do something to experience her promise. All I heard from her was, *"Trust me!"*

Well, at 6:00 p.m. she told me to turn on the television. When I did, the news was just coming on and they were announcing, "The Soviet Union no longer exists." I sat spellbound as the story unfolded. Mary said, *"This is my miracle. It was for the whole world. Did you think it was just for you?"* (She said this with humor.) Then she continued, *"This would not have happened without divine intervention.*

It is part of God's plan for the salvation of mankind."

I sat in amazement, listening outwardly to the news and inwardly to Our Lady. She further said *"My plan can come about only with the aid of your prayers and sacrifices. I need all of my children to listen and respond, for the time is so short until the Father calls me home again. Please spread my messages and live them."*

"I am your Mother. Thank you for responding to my call."

7. The Visionary's Personal Experiences   DEC. 15, 1991

Miracle of the Sun

After returning from Mass this morning, I witnessed the miracle of the sun, an event that is so much talked about these days as happening in Medjugorje. This was totally unexpected and overwhelming.

When I was driving home and pulled up at a stop sign, dark clouds parted, and the brilliant sun, directly in front of me, was covered with a shadow disk (like a host) and was edged in spinning fire. Then colors seemed to shoot out in circular motions, and the sun seemed to spin.

I stopped at my daughter's house, and her husband witnessed this phenomenon with me out in their yard. I called another daughter and told her to go outside and look in the sky, and she and her husband both witnessed the miracle of the sun.

It was cloudy that day, and we put on sunglasses, and the sun did not hurt our eyes at all until the shadow disappeared. Then we couldn't look at the sun at all.

Special note: Fr. Rinfret, in Maryland (her land) had told me earlier on the phone that on December 8, he and several members of his prayer group had witnessed the miracle of the sun and had thought this was the miracle Our Lady had promised for December 8.

8. The Visionary's Personal Experiences   MARCH 17, 1992

A Non-Catholic's Story
A Visit With the Blessed Virgin

The night of March 17, 1992, a friend and I, on the spur of the moment, decided to see her daughter's new home. She lived near another mutual friend's home where we had been visiting, and which was quite a distance from my home. Away we went at 11:00 p.m.

My friend's daughter and her husband were happy to see us and show me their new home. It was all so beautiful and peaceful. My friend asked if we could take a walk on their land. It was fine with them. They were going to bed. My friend had seen a vision of the Virgin Mary, as had several others in her family, and she wanted me to see her, too, there on their land.

It was a medium cold night without a star in the sky for light. There was woods all around. We walked and walked further back in the woods. It's strange, but we could see the small gravel road very clearly and had no problem following it. We finally came up a small hill, and in front of us we could see a high, flat, level field encircled by small and large trees. It was like an arena in the woods. My friend pointed to the place they had seen the Blessed Mother twice before. I turned around, and there she was.

This was a high, big vision of the Virgin Mary standing right in front of my eyes. She was so huge, so beautiful and so gorgeous with a large halo of light over her head. I thought I was going crazy. It didn't seem as if it could be real. This beautiful lady was standing in front of me. I am not even Catholic. How can this be? I have never seen her before—only in pictures and statues. And yet, there she was, right in front of my eyes.

My friend turned to me, and together we started to pray. We repeated the Lord's prayer over and over. Here we were, two women standing in an open field, late at night, praying. I wondered if we had lost our minds. I thought that we had to be nuts.

My friend asked Our Lady to show us a sign that she was really there. All of a sudden, the wind started blowing, but only just across our faces. I was in an unbelievable state of mind—not aware of anything else in the whole world. The wind came, and I opened my mouth to inhale the cold air that was blowing.

Let me state here that we don't look upon ourselves as crazy. We are merely normal, everyday women. We have lived our lives raising our families and living fairly normal, average lives. I have never experienced anything like this.

We continued to stand and pray. We sang hymns and breathed the air blowing on our faces. The air had a scent of lovely fresh flowers. Our faces felt frozen, but when we touched them, they were very warm.

Our Lady talked to us. At one time, her husband, Saint Joseph, stood behind her, and she held the Baby Jesus in her arms out to us. She told us to bring all the children unto God to work with her, as our youth in America are "losing ground." She said that they are going astray. She asked us to lead all the unbelievers unto her and that she would transform them and melt their hearts.

Then angels, appearing as a very bright light, seemed to form around her on both sides. The vision was so beautiful and so powerful that we couldn't move. We felt as if we were dreaming or in another place, another time. We didn't know where we were or what we were doing or even what was going on.

We remained in the state of transfixion for two hours. The time went by like two seconds.

When we started to leave and return back to our car, I found that I could hardly walk. I felt like a person who couldn't stand up—and yet so joyously happy. I was staggering, and my legs were giving out from under me. I was so happy and laughing so hard that I could hardly get my breath. Nothing was funny, but I just kept laughing from happiness.

We got into the car, and then out came the biggest full moon we had ever seen in our lives. We got out of the car and stood beside it. It seemed that the presence of God was right there with us. As we stood by the car, the moon put on the most beautiful show for us. It got huge and very bright and large, and then it got small. It went around and around in slow motion, then in fast motion, traveling faster and faster. It had brilliant colors around it—red, pink, yellow, blue. It came down to us where we could almost reach out and touch it. It was so beautiful and wonderful.

We finally got home, and the moon was right over us. We felt so good and so happy that no one can get near us. We seemed to be removed from reality. We had just spent three wonderful hours with Our Lord and the Blessed Virgin, His mother. God had made us true believers.

I will be changed for the rest of my life here on earth and will do whatever God wills for me.

I am writing this the day after while my mind is clear and fresh with the things and feelings I experienced.

9. The Visionary's Personal Experiences   MAY 9, 1992

At Notre Dame Conference

On Sat. May 9, 1992, while at the Medjugorje Conference at Notre Dame University, I had this personal experience. I am recording it because Our Lady directed me and for my own record.

The picture of Our Lady of Medjugorje that was on the curtain behind the stage appeared to come alive and Our Lady related many messages to me—some personal and some for all.

There was a "golden light" of an angel behind her and when Mass started—the angel turned and knelt, facing the altar.

Our Lady asks that September 1 be designated as Our Lady of Light—the date of her first appearance as such (at the farm in Indiana).

She wants all mothers—to bring their children to her and to consecrate them to her.

She wants the "Our Lady of Light" prayer—that she gave to me—delivered all over the United States. It is to be her first movement here beginning as Our Lady of Light in this country.

Personal observation: Our Lady was crying and it tore at my heart. She further asked me why I had not honored her request as she needed my help. She again asked me to surrender my will to God so that she could use me in her work here in America.

I had never seen Our Lady cry before. It was painful. I, of course, accepted. I will do whatever she directs.

To continue—Our Lady would turn and open her eyes and raise her arms to all the people there. In looking at the people, she was crying. When I asked her why she was crying, she said it was for all the lost souls—especially here in America—and that we all needed to pray for these lost souls, and we should all offer up all of our suffering with

Jesus, her Son, for their salvation. She said even our frustrations and disappointments would be a great offering.

She said she desired that September 1 be a day of prayer. She said on September 1, she would send a sign for all the unbelievers. She said she would be sending me messages she wanted delivered to her prayer groups.

She asked that the children form prayer groups—even in schools—and said to even go to the non-Catholics spreading her messages, as they are also her children. She desires each family to form family prayer groups and to pray together, for through prayer and through prayer groups, she can do much. She reminds us that we are **all** her family. She said all of our suffering—all of our disappointments, all of our lives—should be dedicated to her and her Son.

She said Satan is very strong at this time—especially with the youth and the youth (especially of our country) need her help and our help.

She is calling all mothers to rally to her aid.

She is calling on us as a mother to mothers. She said that united, the mothers can change the world. We mothers, especially, should all look to her for help, and she will tell each of us—in our hearts—what each of us are to do.

She said many calamities are about to befall the earth, and all that is taking place across the seas will spill over into our land and we will need her help to overcome this and to deal with it.

If we do not listen to her call—many more things will happen.

Note: I also saw Jesus on the cross. He looked real but did not look at me. His body was covered with blood. Our Lady said, *"This is for the sins of the world."*

Our Lady also said she desired that the churches be open everywhere so that the people can go in and worship. She said there is no need to close her churches, for God does not want to lock the people out.

She said that God wants them to be able to come to Him at any time and as this is His house—and we are simply its caretakers—we should honor this request and let the doors remain open.

10. The Visionary's Personal Experiences   MAY 10, 1992

Mother's Day at Notre Dame

Our Lady said that because we were honoring her with our presence on Mother's Day, instead of bringing honor to ourselves by staying home with our own families, this was her gift to us and said, "Happy Mothers Day."

She was holding a cross of golden light in each hand and extended them to my friend and I, asking us to accept these crosses (a commitment to her). My friend and I both accepted, and the crosses disappeared.

She had so many messages—and I will try to recall each one of them here.

She said we must pray hard—for the time is not any longer "short"—but is **now**. The cup of chastisement was now spilling on the earth. She said she needed our help as much as we needed hers.

She is calling on all mothers everywhere on this Mother's Day, to join her in her battle so that she can triumph in her mission here. Without us, she can do nothing. She said the mothers of the world united with her can save mankind.

She asks us to bring our children and all children to her—to consecrate the children and all of the youth to her Immaculate Heart and the Sacred Heart of Jesus, for they are especially the target of Satan at this time. They are weak and need our strength to overcome these temptations.

She wants us to form prayer groups and to start them in the schools—to have family prayers, and community prayers. This will bring about peace once again. It must be started in each individual, each community, and spread out to join other communities. Only in this way can it be effective and enduring. This will be our sign to her that we are sincere.

She asks that we not be bored with her so easily, for she has come to guide us and give us hope, but we refuse to cooperate.

She said that if her wishes and messages are not carried out, she will not come again.

She advises that we are much like children who receive a new gift which thrill them but after awhile discard it in pursuit of some other new pleasure.

She is begging and pleading with us not to abandon her

now and to join our efforts with hers, for there is little time now as it has come upon us. She said, *"Do not delay or you will be lost. I cry for all of my lost children."*

She has come to crush the head of the serpent, which is the evil in all mankind, but she needs our help and our wills, so we must choose.

She wishes September 1 to be designated as a day of prayer to Our Lady of Light. She wants the prayer "Our Lady of Light" to be distributed throughout the United States.

She also stated that she will appear at midnight in St. Joseph Church (Kentucky) on September 1 (actually at midnight on August 31) and wished us to be with her then. She said it was her plan that her statue be sent to this church, for she sent it there. It was not an accident of fate, and it was no coincidence.

She asked that Fr. Smith of this parish be approached and asked to be her special servant and to aid her in the work she wishes to accomplish here. She said we do not have to convince him of anything as she will take care of that. He is a very special son to her, and she knows he will respond to her as he has in the past. She said to remind him of—*"the golden cross."* To tell him that his love for her shall be rewarded, and his efforts have not gone unnoticed by her or her Son.

She said she has recruited Father Rinfret in the eastern section of America and now calls on Father Smith to accept her invitation here in the middle section. She stated that another priest shall be called upon and added from the western section of America, and these three would be her special ambassadors here in America.

She stated that these are her wishes, but she does not insist, she only asks that each one accepts of his own free will.

I will do as she directed me, for I know now that she will guide and help me.

To go on with our experience, when Jesus was appearing, He pointed His arm and finger up and to the left. When I looked to see where He pointed, I didn't understand. Then He raised His arm and pointed straight up and said, *"The Father."*

He also imparted to me that we should all pray more to

our Heavenly Father, not only to Him and His Mother. And also said that these visions here were allowed and sent by The Father—as a special grace, as was the gift of His Mother at this time to help **all** of mankind.

I have promised her that I would carry out the wishes she is asking of me. That is why I am writing of it and will share it with whomever she so directs me.

11. The Visionary's Personal Experiences   MAY 30, 1992

For Documentation

On May 30, 1992, at St. Joseph Church in Kentucky, I met my aunt and a friend, to hear a lecture on healing from a man and lady from Arizona.

While praying the rosary with the crowd, I suddenly saw Our Lady come to life in her statue. She raised her head and looked at us and smiled, just like she was sort of acknowledging us.

She smiled, and then put her head down, and was gone.

This only lasted a few minutes. My friend and I both saw her.

I am writing this to document occurences of these past days as Our Lady has directed me to do. I am not trying to prove anything to anyone; I am merely a servant of Our Lady trying to do her wishes.

Our Lady had told me she would send a sign to both her priests (Fr. Smith and Fr. Rinfret) on Ascension Day. I told both of them this information (by mail).

On Friday morning I was in a sea of doubt, and I asked Our Lady to please help me to give me some sign from her to erase these feelings.

I asked, "If these priests have been given a sign of some kind, will you please let me know about it?"

It wasn't five minutes later that Fr. Smith called me to relate, "I think I got my sign from Our Lady."

As I listened, he went on to explain that he had received a call from another priest in Cincinnati (that he didn't know) telling him what had happened at St. Joseph Church the preceding evening.

This priest told him that two people were presently in his office and verified it. It seems a young girl at the church had seen the statue of Mary come to life and smile at her. She said it frightened her at first. She also saw Jesus, and in place of the crown of flowers on the statue of Mary, Jesus was wearing a crown of thorns.

Needless to say, I was uplifted as this was my sign also that Our Lady was truly at work here.

That isn't all though. Last night at the church, I asked Fr. Smith if he had heard of anything unusual happening to Fr. Rinfret that could have been from Our Lady.

He said that Fr. Rinfret told him that during Mass a lady mystic, with whom he had been assisting as spiritual advisor, experienced the stigmata; her palms showed signs of bleeding.

So, I do truly believe that Our Lady fulfilled her promise and sent powerful messages to "her" priests.

12. The Visionary's Personal Experiences   JULY 9, 1992

The Miracle of the Moon

This evening, several members of my family witnessed what we refer to as "the miracle of the moon." Five of us saw a rainbow around the moon and then a cross of light covering it. At times, the rainbow would spin.

I called Fr. Smith to tell him to observe the moon to see if it appeared this way to him. I felt this was some sign from Our Lady since T.V. news was going to report this evening about her promise to appear at St. Joseph Church on September 1. I felt this was a sign from Our Lady to remind us that she had her hand in this occurrence also.

After the 11 p.m. news telling the story of St. Joseph Church, I felt somewhat overwhelmed and started mentally asking Our Lady, "Oh, my goodness, what have you asked of me, and what have you gotten me into here—T.V. coverage and thousands of people?"

As her answer, the five members of my family who witnessed the rainbow on the moon all felt a strong urge to go to my daughter's field nearby where Our Lady had appeared many times before to many of us.

It was a stormy night with lots of lightning. However, we followed our urge and went.

When we arrived, we could see Our Lady of Light in the trees where she had been before. She was a figure of light, and told us not to fear the lightning, that she would protect us. Those present were my daughter and three of my grand-daughters (all young teenagers). It started to rain lightly, but none of us got wet.

Our Lady gave us many personal messages and then assured me that all that was happening was in her plans and that I should remember that she will handle all the things I am concerned about and not to worry anymore. She asked me (again) to surrender myself totally to God's will so that I would not experience any misgivings again.

We prayed together, and she became brighter. When the lightning flashed, we could see her more clearly. One of my granddaughters (age 11) was seeing her for the first time. We heard a baby crying. I was told that this was the Baby Jesus (although we did not see Him), and He was crying because of the evil in our world and the sins of mankind.

My other two granddaughters were crying, too, as Our Lady had given them many personal messages which touched their hearts. She asked them to be examples to other youth and to lead them back to Jesus.

We thanked her for everything she had given us, and Our Lady left. When we got into our car, it started storming and raining very hard, but when we got back to my home, the rain stopped completely. We never got wet, even in the midst of the storm.

13. The Visionary's Personal Experiences   AUG. 3, 1992

A Walk in the Field

This evening, my daughter and I went for a walk in her field, and on returning to her house, I saw Our Lady in the trees (as a shadow of light).

She was holding the Baby Jesus in her right arm and was just looking down at Him.

There were three other figures of light around her which I somehow "knew" were angels.

My daughter saw this "light" but could not distinguish any figures.

14. The Visionary's Personal Experiences   AUG. 11, 1992

A Wonderful Visit with Our Lady

At about 9:30 p.m., I went to my daughter's home where I had seen Our Lady before, because I had this strong urge to go there. My other daughter and her husband, as well as my niece and her daughter, decided to join me, and we all met there. We walked back in the field and all of us saw Our Lady of Light there in the trees.

At first, just my son-in-law and I walked back there before the others came out in the field. It was then that my son-in-law saw her for the first time. He saw her move and turn and get brighter and bigger. She was near the ground but then slowly rose up to the tree-top level. She turned toward the house and blessed it and then turned toward us and blessed us.

She answered my son-in-law's questions (through me) and also gave me many personal messages. She was crying at one point, and tears were flowing down her left cheek. She was crying over so many lost souls and so many more that would be lost. She said we should pray and fast to stop the wars. She said our land would soon feel the cup of chastisement, and we should pray that it would be lightened.

I asked her to send a sign for those who needed one, to show that she was really there. Shortly after, she turned sideways and motioned for us to go out further in the field, which we did. At this time, there were seven of us present.

There was a full moon, and it was very bright, and there were "flashes of light" everywhere (this happens often when Our Lady appears), and there was a shooting star that seemed to "bounce" across the sky. Then a large light appeared over the tree tops and seemed to go up and down and sway back and forth. Flashes of colored lights seemed to come from it, and then it just rose slowly until it was out of sight. We all felt this was Our Lady's sign to us. My other son-in-law had joined us by that time and also witnessed this sign.

15. The Visionary's Personal Experiences   AUG. 16, 1992

She Called a Meeting

Today an unplanned and unexpected beautiful experience happened. My daughter called and asked if I would like to go with (her and her husband) to visit the farm where we first saw Our Lady of Light (September 1, 1991). I agreed and went with them.

After we got there, another lady friend phoned and said she had a strong urge to call. When she found out we were all there, she decided to come and asked if she could bring another friend with her. So they joined us there at the farm.

Now, strange as it may seem, this put together again the original five ladies who saw Our Lady of Light on September 1, 1991, and it was the first time since then.

Naturally, after it got dark, we all went out to the field where she had first appeared. This time, however, there were two more with us, my son-in-law and my other daughter. All of us present had seen Our Lady at different times and places.

Well, Our Lady undoubtedly arranged all of us being there (almost like she had called a meeting) and needless to say, she blessed all of us with her presence once again. It was all so beautiful.

This time she was in a different spot, but still a figure of light in the trees. She called us to come closer and to pray with her. We prayed the Rosary with her and asked her what she wanted of us.

She asked that each of us individually "accept" to do her wishes. All of us said "yes" out loud. She did not say what she wanted of us—only that we accept.

She was crying at one point, and I cried with her. It was so sad to see Our Lady cry.

At one time another figure of light was to her right and I could see Jesus in it. Our Lady was then turned toward Him and was kneeling. All of us saw this, and all of us also saw lights of angels surrounding the field. One was especially bright, and when I asked who it was, I was told it was "Gabriel."

She was there from around 9:30 p.m. until 11:00. Again,

this time passed fast, as it always seems time "stands still" whenever she appears.

I, of course, said (in the beginning of her appearance, as I always do), "If you are not from the Lord, you are not welcome here." Then I sprinkled holy water around the area. Our Lady just smiled and said, *"Come closer."*

At one time, she left the trees and came down close to the ground. She had her arms outstretched to us. Again, I asked her for a sign that it was really her. Shortly after that a huge ball (like lightning) was on the right of us and suddenly shot across the field and actually passed through my son-in-law and me. It felt like a jolt of electricity and it seemed to lift us off the ground. We both yelled out because it was so strong a feeling. Her signs are tremendous and overwhelming. I feel this was the Holy Spirit because of some of the personal messages she had given to each of us.

Also, from the time we got there in the field, there were the mysterious flashes of light all over the area.

I think that this was the sign she promised for August 15, but due to outside interference, we could not get there until the next day. I learned later that they had talked about going on Saturday, the 15th, but then waited until Sunday to go.

I am writing this for my own record and because Our Lady requested me to. Once again, I am not trying to prove anything to anyone, I am just grateful to be chosen for such a great blessing.

16. The Visionary's Personal Experiences

Questions and Answers

Many people may have questions in their minds concerning the appearance of "Our Lady of Light" at this time. The following questions were asked of the visionary.

Q. How do you see Our Lady?
A. I, as well as others, see her as a figure of light. However, on several occasions, I have seen her as a real three dimensional being, shimmering in a great light.
Q. How do you hear her?
A. I hear her inwardly and not an actual voice. I seem to

be able to hear her thoughts, even when she directs them to others.

Q. How do you know these visions are of God and not the devil?

A. Any time she appears, I always say (mentally), "If you are not from the Lord, you are not welcome, and be gone." Our Lady will sometimes answer, *"I am from the Lord,"* but at other times will simply smile and look pleased.

Q. How do you know you are relating her messages correctly?

A. I do not write her messages during her appearances, but write them later. I seem to recall them as she spoke them, but if there is a doubt, I will ask for clarification from her.

Q. Why do you remain anonymous?

A. Because Our Lady wishes me to "be invisible" for now. She has said many times, it is her messages that are important and not her messenger.

Q. How do you know when the messages are from Our Lady and when they are from Jesus?

A. The inner messages I receive are recognizable by the voice sending it, and they will tell me who they are when the message is ended.

Q. Does Our Lady have a special day or time to appear to you?

A. No. She comes to me at different times and different places. There is no set time or date by her.

Q. How does she arrive, and how to you know when she is coming?

A. She will announce her appearances by flashes of light, and these flashes will continue during her apparition.

Q. Has Our Lady revealed any secrets to you that are to be revealed later?

A. I cannot comment on this. But Our Lady always says to *"carry hope and not fear."*

Q. How do you know which messages are "personal" (for you only) and which are for all?

A. Some personal messages also include messages to be shared by all. Therefore, I have released all of these to both priests, but there are others that were meant and directed only to me, and those I have kept to myself. I can tell by the content if the messages are just for me.

17. The Visionary's Personal Experiences

Lady of Light

Oh, Lady of Light—
Shining so bright—
Be with us this day
Guiding our way
Oh, Lady of Light!

Oh, beautiful Lady,
Glowing so bright,
Your eyes softly beaming
And gleaming with light.

Oh, wonderful Mother,
I feel you so near.
Your presence dissolves
All of my fears.

Your comforting arms
Reach out to all
Your gentle voice whispers
A low pleading call.

You wait there so patient—
And keep us in sight.
Thank You, Dear Mother,
"Our Lady of Light!"

The visionary was awakened in the middle of the night and given these words by Our Lady.

LADY OF LIGHT

M. A. CROWLEY

Chapter III

Ave Maria—Our Lady's Requests

1. Our Lady's Request   OCT. 28, 1991

To the People of America

I am your Mother and wish to be known in America as "The Lady of Light." For America is in spiritual darkness which they have created through their ignorance of the errors of their ways.

I have come to America now so that I can help them in their search through this spiritually blinding time and to lead them into the light of God.

Oh, America! My heart is saddened when I view you, for you have completely shut your God out of your lives and gone off in selfish pursuit of your own selfish desires. Now is the time you must choose. Are you for my Son, or shall you ignore His tender pleading to surrender yourself to Him so that He can heal you?

If you continue to turn away and insult your Maker, you will draw serious consequences upon you and your land.

You have been given much, and therefore, your responsibility is also one of abundance. When you see a need, do you always fill it?

And when you do, for what purpose? Is it to truly befriend and help your neighbor, or are your intentions in helping them for your own selfish reasons? Examine your conscience, and remember, you cannot fool your God, for He sees into your heart. Give freely and expect nothing in return.

36

I, as your Mother, see my children squabbling over their possessions, and I am trying to teach you to share fairly.

You are in darkness now, but if you will follow me, The Light, I shall lead you into a brighter future. I am asking you to change your lives and convert before it is too late, but you must desire this and choose it or it will not happen.

My heart is saddened when I look at your churches and cathedrals. They are beautiful to the eye and certainly draw attention to the great workmanship that was employed here. But where are the worshiping faithful of my Son?

True, many people may come into such magnificent structures, but merely to comment on the artful designs therein, and not to worship their Lord and God.

No one seems to care that their Lord and Friend sits lonely in your church houses waiting for you to call. Why have you turned away from Him when He has given you so much?

Don't you see what you are doing? You are creating a barrier between the Creator and you, His creation. I implore you to reconcile with your God. Do it now, for tomorrow may be too late. The time on His clock grows shorter. Pray, convert and put peace back into your lives as it was meant to be.

I see your temptations and I know your weaknesses, but if you will consecrate yourself to me and my Immaculate Heart, together we shall produce a victory, and you will be free once again to walk again in the company of your Lord and God, and you will be strangers no more.

I come to you now, with a mother's love, and remind you that you are walking on a wrong path. I implore you to let me help you. I will shine my love and my light into your soul if you only permit me.

Please give me your heart so that I might help you remold it into one of unconditional love. It is my desire and the desire of my Son that you be happy with us into eternity.

Thank you for responding to my call.

2. Our Lady's Request   **NOV. 18, 1991**

Pray More and Talk Less

People are only talking about my messages and not doing them and practicing them in their daily lives. They must be examples to those who do not believe.

People are only talking about praying but doing very little in their daily routines. I wish them to pray more and talk less.

People are searching for me and my Son in holy places and far away places, and neglecting to seek Us in the stillness of their soul, where We are already residing.

I wish my children to purify their hearts and to listen for their own small still voice to direct them in the mission that is for them.

I need my faithful souls, all of them. For only with their help can I accomplish the purification and the salvation for mankind.

Thank you for responding to my call.

3. Our Lady's Request　　　　　NOV. 21, 1991

To the Priests

I wish all priests to realize that your Holy Mother and Jesus are real.

We are not some mystical Ghosts or spirit form—in some far-off place. We are here "among" you—And we are real!

Portray This to the People in Your Charge

I also desire that you introduce me to your non-Catholic brethren. They have been misinformed about me and my role as their mother. I need you to help me open their hearts to my motherly love.

I am here on earth today to help all of my children return to God.

Thank you for responding to my call.

4. Our Lady's Request　　　　　FEB. 9, 1992

The Scriptures are Continuing

A sign shall be sent on March 3 (1992), so that you will believe. It is a time of miracles and much blessing for mankind.

The scriptures have not stopped but are continuing even more so in these days and times.

They should be recorded for future generations and as testimony to the great manifestations of the handiwork of the Almighty.

It is of these times that history on your planet will be completed and also begun. The signs are now upon you. The scriptures are unfolding and also being rewritten. [In the sense of being written again.]

To those of you who stored your wealth in the physical domain of worldly possessions, there will be much wailing and crying. But to those who gave of themselves and shared with their fellow man all they had, a day of great rejoicing will be upon them, for the Lord God has deemed it so, and these shall receive their spiritual treasures.

I thank you for answering my call. I am your mother. [*Editor's Note:* Our Lady explained later on.]

SEPT. 15, 1992

My child, your Holy Scriptures are being rewritten, in that they have not concluded but are being rewritten with continuing revelations and ongoing experiences that should thus be recorded and added to the Holy Scriptures that have already transpired and already have been divinely recorded.

I am your mother and thank you for your response.

[*Editor's Comments:* The above messages at first strike a chord of concern. The Holy Scriptures, the Bible, together with the Tradition of the Church constitute Its divine authority. The Scriptures closed with the death of John, the last apostle. The public revelation of the Bible, itself somewhat based on what might today be called private revelation, is sufficient in and of itself.

However, when one reads Our Lady's request carefully, a different perspective is gained. She is not indicating change or documentation for needs of salvation. Our Lady is very positive. She is speaking of the eventful and important days ahead. The Scriptures were opened for the life of Jesus and His Apostles to record the events and give us the light of Christ. Her request is that they now be opened again to document a new frame of reference, a new era.

Bear in mind that this is one of her first public messages here as if to set the stage for what was to follow. She also specifically asked at this time that her messages be referred to as "Her Requests." She is making this request for purposes of recording history for future generations.

One may wonder from these requests that there will be an important era ahead, a time of epoch events, possibly a time of much wailing and great rejoicing. Does the "much wailing" refer to a corrective process, a purification, a chastisement? Could it be a period of apostasy or a period of spiritual darkness, or of persecution? Could it allude to a warning perhaps? And what about the "great rejoicing and these shall receive their spiritual treasures"? What spiritual treasures are to be recorded for future generations? One can only speculate in regard to specifics but there may be those who conclude that major happenings in Heaven's time are soon to occur. A clarifying statement was made later by Our Lady which we have extracted from a personal message as follows.]

OCT. 26, 1992

My child, I pointed out to you that in Fatima during the early part of this century, I also came as "Our Lady of Light," and the reference to the "New Era" had already begun even then. All of my appearances, then and since then, are connected together, for I am the same Lady, and my messages are the same. As at Fatima, so it is now. You are thinking in man's time, not God's. Be patient, for all shall unfold on schedule, but in God's time.

Know that all of my appearances in every part of the earth are part of a plan for the salvation of mankind. It is, therefore, requested that all should be recorded and retained. Yes, these will be the additional scriptures. Both "private" and "public" appearances are necessary to draw my children back to God, so both are important and should be recorded. In the discernment of these appearances, you shall know the truth by the forthcoming fruits of each event. The truth shall be revealed in the bearing of the fruit.

5. Our Lady's Request   FEB. 9, 1992

The Catholic Church Should Be the Catalyst

I am reaching out to many of my faithful souls at this time because many workers are needed to harvest the souls in danger of loss, but the number are few that respond. I am grateful for your acceptance—all of my responding souls.

I desire that the Catholic Church should be the catalyst to unite all faithful souls under one roof. It is the time of fulfillment of many Scriptures as well as the unfoldment of my messages to my children on earth through the " Fatima Messages."

I urge all of you to continue to pray my Rosary and to urge all of your brothers and sisters to do so also.

In this way, I can continue to intervene and forestall, if not eliminate, the catastrophic events to befall earth as a chastisement for their errors.

It is not the Father's plan or desire to do this, but mankind has brought these events upon himself by his pride and greed. Pray that these demons be destroyed in each individual and that peace be restored in each heart.

I have given you the means and shown you the way, but you do not budge. I plead with you to take my messages seriously, for the time grows short.

The grace of the Father has permitted me to be with you and help you, but many of you refuse my extended hand. Many of you speak whole words, but many of your deeds are merely actions of false motives.

I assure you that the Father sees into your hearts and sees what your true intentions are. I desire that you make your intentions pure of heart so that they will go directly to the Father.

You must rid yourselves of falsehoods and live a life that is united with God. You cannot walk two roads any longer. You must now choose. If you are not for God then you shall be against Him. If you are for Him then give yourself fully to Him—your possessions, all of your desires— and relinquish your will to do His Holy Will. Open yourselves to the healing ointment of God's unconditional love so that you may bloom fruitfully and abundantly.

Above all else, I desire that you love one another, even as God, your Father, has loved you, for He has given you life and your free will. What have you, dear children, given to your Father?

I desire that you quit judging your brothers and sisters, or you shall bring judgment on yourselves.

I desire that you quit looking with contempt on those less fortunate than you. Remember, what you do to the least of your brethren, you do also to your God.

I desire that you quit raising yourselves above others, for in the family of God, of which you are a part (a most important part), there are non "better" and none "less."

I also desire that you quit holding resentments and grudges against each other. These practices will stain your spirit and separate you from the peace you were given by the Creator and will separate you from your Creator.

Remember, dear children, you cannot come to the Father if you harbor these impurities in your spirit. You must have a pure heart so that you present no falsehood. You must learn to pray with all your heart and all your might. For a prayer from a pure heart is stronger than any force you know on earth. So purify your hearts and prepare before you approach the Father. Thus, you will have the assurance of union with Him.

My children, if you do not speak to your Creator now, how will He know you when you come into the spiritual world before Him? I urge you to start now. It is never too late, and there is nothing you have done or will do that has not already been forgiven you through the death of my Son, Jesus, on the Cross.

I am your Mother, and I want all of you, my children, to be with me in Heaven. My call goes forth to every corner of the earth. Please listen—I beg of you!

Pray, fast, convert and reconcile with one another. I urge you to consecrate yourselves to my Immaculate Heart and to the Sacred Heart of my Son.

Do not waste your time, for it is running out. I urge you to be a Child of God, and start today to love one another.

I am your mother. Thank you for answering my call. Please continue to spread my messages for they are converting many souls.

When asked by another what they can do, tell them to live my messages and be examples to others of how to live a holy life.

6. Our Lady's Request   MARCH 17, 1992

Give Me Your Hearts

Give me your hearts and I shall transform them for you. Do not stay detached from your God but unite your will to His Will and you will find peace.

I have come so that you know Me, for I am your Mother. I ask that all who suffer offer their pain along with my Son's agony on the Cross for the atonement of my lost children.

I bring hope to those of you who are lost and confused. I wish to shed light into your darkened world and lead you back to my Son. But, you must desire this, or it will not happen.

I urge you to open your hearts like the budding flower so that you may receive the graces sent you by the Father.

If you remain closed and will not listen, then these graces will flow with no purpose.

Open your hearts so that you will be able to receive God's abundant love.

Pray! Pray! Pray every day, every minute and make your life a prayer so that you will never know doubts and your faith will be strong.

In your sorrow and pain—
I am here—

In your doubts and confusion—
I am here—

In your day and your night—
I am here—

In your grief and loneliness—
I am here—

Ever so near.

You are my children, and I am your Mother. Thank you for your response.

7. Our Lady's Request   **APRIL 18, 1992**

As One Mother to Another

I am the Lady of Light and have come to shed light unto your darkened world.

Open your hearts to my love so that you may be filled with the Holy Spirit.

I am urging all mothers to bring their children to my open

arms, for I have much love to give them. I am pleading for the salvation of my dear children, for they have been abandoned. No one is tending the children and they have fallen under the destructive forces of the devil. Many in this land are even openly worshiping this false god and are in greater need than ever of my mother's mantle to protect them from this evil influence.

I implore you, as one mother to another, to come to my aid. Our children are at stake. Introduce them to me so that I may lead them to my Son, Jesus.

Have them pray the Rosary and form rosary groups—yes, even in their schools, for there is corruption there also. I will guide my children and then they can guide their counterparts and other children who have lost their way. Satan's power is strong and they, the children, cannot battle it alone.

Form groups and I shall join you in your prayers. In this way we can divert the tactics of Satan.

In daily Masses, I desire that the seven Our Fathers, seven Hail Marys and seven Glory Bes be intoned at its conclusion, for my special intentions. I implore you to do this so that I can enact my plan of peace here in America.

My dear children, I need you, and you need my help. That is why I have come to you. I wish to lead you out of your darkness, but you, yes, even my faithful ones, refuse to follow.

By your actions and inactions you are preparing a bitter cup. If you do not respond to my messages and convert your way of living, you will have to drink it.

Do not be mistaken and drawn in by the false promises of Satan and do not presume you are above the retribution of your chosen errors. You have chosen unwisely in the past. Now you must choose again. Continue on your path of destruction, or turn back to your God and Creator. I am here to help you, my children.

Thank you for answering my call. I am your Mother.

8. Our Lady's Request

[*Visionary's Comments:* Our Lady wanted me to approach all mothers and ask for their help. I told her I would not know how to approach all the mothers. She said to not worry, that she would give me a letter, and she did. Here it is.

She wants it distributed and put in the hands of all mothers everywhere. She said she will then be able to touch their hearts and melt them. She also thanks them for responding to her call.]

Calling all Mothers

Mothers of the world, unite! It's time for changes and we have it in our power to be effective tools to bring about these changes.

We must restore our families to a throne of dignity. The family life has fallen by the wayside, and our society is now paying the cost.

Look around you. The whole world is in utter chaos. There are growing numbers of our brothers and sisters becoming completely homeless and hopeless. They have lost their way and need our help. All of these people have a mother that cries in her heart over this dilemma. Then, too, some of them are mothers and have no way to care for their children. Can we, as mothers, turn our eyes away and turn deaf ears to their pleas for help?

You may say, "Yes, I know, but what can I do? I'm just an individual." That is true, but if we join hands, mothers, we can sweep the country and the world with a tidal wave of aid and comfort to all who are in need.

How can we sit undisturbed and unnoticing in our comfortable niche and witness these atrocities that are taking place all around us? How can we, as mothers, watch other mothers suffer because their children are suffering? In a sense, aren't **all** mothers in charge of ALL children not only our own?

In Ireland, several years back, two mothers stopped a raging war between the Catholics and Protestants because they had seen enough and had had enough of watching their sons and family members being slaughtered for the evils of power and greed. They went door to door and approached other mothers. They made the difference.

And you still ask, "what measly portion of help will my efforts make?"

There are not only homeless situations that need correcting, but our whole country and our whole world is a sick child calling for the comforting hand of its mother. As a wise soul and leader of man once said, ''The hand that rocks the cradle, rocks the world!''

He was right!

As one mother to another, I urge you to throw away your apathy and start to care again. Do Something!

Examine your heart and seek a need that you can fill. Ask God to guide you. I know you'll get an answer, if you'll only ask, ''What can I do?''

I'll tell you what you can do, mothers of the world, you can change it.

Thank you for your response.

A Mother.

9. Our Lady's Request   MAY 20, 1992

A Sign Shall Be Sent

My Child,

On Thursday, May 28, Ascension Thursday, I shall send the Holy Spirit to strengthen your spirit and enable you to go forward in peaceful surrender and with quiet strength.

Know that my Son is walking with you.

My two chosen priests, Fr. Rinfret and Fr. Smith, shall have the Holy Spirit descend on them on this day also and will know what they are to do. This shall happen at the consecration of the Mass.

A sign shall also be sent to each of them, that they may believe.

I am your mother and I thank you for your response.

10. Our Lady's Request   MAY 26, 1992

My Message Has Not Changed

My dear and faithful children,

I do not come to you to entertain you, but to help you. I am not an illusion or a magic trick, but I am your real mother and I'm trying to put you back on your spiritual path. But many of you look on me as a curiosity or an experience to bring you a glimmer of joy to be enjoyed at your convenience.

If you do not take me or my messages seriously, then, I am powerless to help you. I will show you the way and will direct you if you listen and follow.

I came at the beginning of this century to aid you, and I am here at the end to strengthen you, but so many of you refuse to bring light into your darkened world, for you have learned to "like the dark."

My heart bleeds and agonizes over the loss of so many of my children. The time is here that you must choose between darkness and light.

I, as the Queen of this light, have come to many of you either directly or indirectly, and have asked for your allegiance and your help in bringing about my plan of peace for your earth, which I am also a part of. I have a great love for all of you.

My message has not changed, and I am delivering it once more.

Convert your lives back to God, or you shall lose them. Put God first in your daily lives, and be responsible for the free will given you by Him. Many of you have broken your trust with God by thinking you do not need Him and that you are capable of taking care of yourself without Him. In thinking of yourself above God, you have fallen into the same wrongful attitude as the angel Lucifer, who fell from God's grace.

However, there is still time to come home and to rejoin your Father's house. I urge all of you who have become wrapped up in self, to have a change of heart and give yourself back to God, your Father.

I have given you the remedy for achieving this—prayer of the heart. But many of you still only say words without meaning.

In looking on the faithful at Sunday Masses and Sunday services in the churches worldwide, their hearts reveal that they are there out of "obligation" and not out of love. You should be there to honor God, not to please men.

You must correct your steps, for they are leading you away from the peace that was given you. If you only knew how much you are loved, you would not refuse.

I will take you step by step and day by day back to God if you'll let me.

I will lead you to my Son, who died on the Cross for your salvation, if you will surrender your will and give your life totally to Him. Many of you did this, but you also made your own reservations with this commitment and, thus did not really give up your free will to God.

I gave you effective tools to use at the beginning of this century to combat the evils of your world and to refute the devil who was given free reign of your world in this century. I armed you with my Rosary and my Scapular. Now, as at Fatima, use the Rosary and the Scapular to defeat and destroy the wishes of Satan. I will pray with you so that the heavenly Father will surely accept your prayers of faith.

Also now, as at Fatima, you must pray unceasingly and you must fast! I have repeatedly told you that if you would do so, you could stop wars and even control weather conditions. Many of you heard these words but did not accept them as truth.

My children, I urge you now to take your stand beside me, so that together we can move forth. I am pulling for you, but you are tugging away in other directions.

I am here, I am real, and I am near. Come to me.

I am your mother. Thank you for hearing my call.

11. Our Lady's Request   MAY 31, 1992

The Priest in the West

As I have sent a sign to my priest in the east, and my priest in the center, I shall now send a sign to my priest in the west. This shall occur during the Pentecost season and he shall know it has been sent by me.

This priest has already answered my call and is presently doing my work, but I have further need of him to complete my plan here.

If he chooses to accept, you will learn of him soon. You shall not need to approach him, as another has been directed to do so.

There also will be no need to convince him because I shall do this and will ask for his acceptance. But he must choose to accept.

Thank you for answering my call. I am your Mother.

12. Our Lady's Request JUNE 16, 1992

Focus On My Son

My Child, do not be concerned as to earthly appearances. To serve God always brings challenges. The Holy Spirit shall fortify you against these challenges. Be strong in your faith, and know that I, your Mother, am leading you.

Why do you hesitate? Are you ashamed of me? As you have not abandoned me, neither shall I abandon you. Focus on my Son, and your thinking shall not be swayed.

You cannot serve two masters any longer. It does not matter what men may say, as long as you are doing the will of the Father; your actions will find favor with God, your true Father. There have always been unbelievers. I cannot interfere with their free choices and neither can I reach a heart that is closed.

Pray for these souls so they may open their hearts to receive God's abundant graces.

It is a time of special graces from your heavenly Father, as my visits are one of these gifts. But if one is not receptive, they will not receive.

I have come to lead my children back to their spiritual paths and back to God, but many refuse to follow.

To those of you, my children, who have listened and have accepted me, I plead with you not to wander back into your fields of doubt and mistrust, but to stand firm in your faith and be a beacon to your lost brothers and sisters.

I shall continue to intercede for you with my Son, so that all may be saved. Pray, pray, pray and fast. In so doing, you shall not be drawn into the snares of Satan, for he does not want you to acknowledge me, and he does not want me to lead you to my Son.

Consecrate yourselves and all of your families to my Immaculate Heart and to the Sacred Heart of Jesus, my Son. In this way, you will have our protection from the evils of the world.

I have come through the Catholic Church because these are my only children that recognize me and accept me, but even many here also refuse my extended hand. How can I help you if you will not let me?

I remind all, that I am the Mother of all and have come at this time to aid all of you in your trials and sufferings.

Oh, my children, why do you have ears and not hear? Why do you have eyes and not see?

You are destroying yourselves. I beg you to turn back to God, before it is too late. I have told you that the cup of chastisement is now flowing on earth, and it shall touch all of you, the good and the bad, before it evaporates.

What good will exist if you come to possess all of this world and all of its glitter and then destroy your soul?

My children, strive to live a holy life, and you will obtain faith.

Live your life to be an example to others. Helping others is the true way to help yourself.

I am your mother, and I thank you for your response to my call.

13. Our Lady's Request JULY 5, 1992

To Fr. Smith

My Son,

Let not your heart be troubled and your thoughts disturbed by the ways of men, for I, your mother, shall direct your steps and be your comfort. Be of strong faith and stand firmly by my wishes and I shall be your strength.

It is my desire that wherever honor is bestowed in my behalf, that My Son be elevated to even higher honor.

Because you have acknowledged me, I shall now acknowledge you. Carry no doubt and you will observe my presence.

I have chosen you because of your love and devotion. I have chosen your parish because of the faith I find there. Also as it is the church honoring my spouse [St. Joseph].

As you have gone far and wide to seek me and my Son, I shall now come to you to return your favors and to also seek your help. I need many of my faithful souls now more than before. But there are so few who I can turn to. In the beginning, so many came. So many cared, so many chose to answer my call, but now the numbers are few and even the elect have turned away from me and are seeking pleasures and approval of the world. Many have become bored and lost interest in my visits.

The time is short that I have left with you. Please urge

my children to pray and fast. Wars can be stopped and even weather controlled by these means. But they must pray from the heart and must fast for pure and unselfish reasons. They must do this out of love, though, and not out of obligation.

Urge my children to convert their lives and to unite once more with their God. If they have no foundation, their spiritual house [soul] could collapse and they will be lost in darkness.

As you have come to me, why should I not also visit you?

I am your Mother and thank you for your response.

Further messages from Our Lady (for all):

As to your wonderment of the other selected priest in the west, you should practice patience here. It shall be accomplished, not in man's time, but in God's time, and it is still His choice.

In your time of confusion, know that all things are possible with God. You are simply thinking in limits and remember, I have no limits.

If my wishes are accepted, I shall send a gift on August 15.

Stay close to my heart that you do not fall into temptation, for Satan is challenging my plans now with vigor.

14. Our Lady's Request   JULY 10, 1992

I Am The Mother Of All

Tell my children to love one another. They must stop destroying each other and also themselves. They are destroying themselves by their evil actions.

They must forgive their fellow men and be once again what they were designed to be, children of God.

I desire that each of you be filled with the peace of God and be a shining example of God's unconditional love. If you are filled with love, dear children, there will be no room for hatred.

I remind you once again that I am the Mother of *all* and have come to help all of my children. Why will you not open your hearts?

I am your Mother and thank you for your response.

15. Our Lady's Request   JULY 10, 1992

To Fr. Rinfret

My Son,

You have believed while others have not. Know that your faith shall be rewarded. Know that I am ever at your side and shall continue to direct and guide you in your decisions.

You must continue to keep the flame of your faith burning so that others may light theirs from yours.

The signs you have observed and witnessed shall be further testimony of the action of the plans of My Son and me. I need your acceptance to further fulfill my desires.

I have come to help all my children as it is a time of great tribulation, but I need their help also. And I need your help, my son.

As I foretold, I shall send a further sign if my wishes are accepted.

I am your mother, and I thank you for your response.

16. Our Lady's Request   JULY 16, 1992

Focus Totally on Jesus

My child, I urge you not to abandon the path you have chosen. I shall handle any of the troubles foreseen.

I will be your strength. Stand firm in your faith and know that my motherly mantle is protecting you. All that is happening is according to my plan for the salvation of mankind. I have told you that wherever I am, Satan is also and is fighting with vengeance.

Sincere prayer of the heart will keep him from you and in the end, my Immaculate Heart will triumph.

My dear child, I love you and I will not let any harm befall you. If you will carry my wishes, I and my Son will lead you each step. Do not be concerned with what others are saying or doing. Focus totally on Jesus, and you will not be tempted.

I am appearing to many at this time and in many different places. Some are private visits and others are public. Do not be swayed in your faith by other reports. Merely do as I ask and my plan for salvation can move forward.

My Son carries sorrow in His heart because of the

opposition of His people to His mother. He has sent me to help you, but I cannot if I am turned away.

The Holy Spirit has been sent to fortify you and My Son is walking with you.

I thank you for your response. I am your mother.

I shall send a further sign to you August 15.

17. Our Lady's Request   JULY 18, 1992

Make God Your Friend

I am pleased that you have accepted to carry out my wishes. Do not be discouraged by rumors and falsehoods, for these are placed in your path by Satan to deter you from proceeding with the things I am asking of you. I shall place myself between you and Satan, so that he cannot reach you. Remember to **focus** only on Jesus, as He is your companion, and to wear blessed objects, and in this way you shall be uplifted and protected.

For those of my children who have not heard my messages, I urge that they be told of them on September 1. I have chosen this day to be proclaimed in the memory of Our Lady of Light into your darkened world and into the darkened hearts of mankind. I desire also that this church be in dim light for the observance of my presence.

I need my helpers to be strong in their faith. If your faith runs hot and cold you will be swayed away. I urge you to strengthen your faith by prayers of the heart and by fasting. Daily Mass (when possible) and monthly confessions will provide you with a strong armor of faith. Each day, set aside a time to speak with God in the silence of your heart. In this way you will make God your friend and will not feel alienated from Him.

I remind you that I have come to help you, **all** of my children, and I ask that you do not turn a deaf ear to my pleas. Listen to my messages and begin to **live them**.

I am your mother. I thank you for your response.

18. Our Lady's Request   JULY 23 , 1992

Make Peace With Your Secrets

My children, many of you are harboring secrets that are destroying your soul. My children, you have no secrets from

God, for He sees into your soul and knows your every act and every thought.

I urge you now to make peace with your secrets by converting your lives. My children, you must make peace with your secrets before you can make peace with your God. Look into your soul and purify it of anything there that is not holy. In this way, you are opening your heart, and thus God's love and grace can enter.

Jesus, my Son, has made you this promise: *"Come to Me, you who are weary, and I shall refresh you and give you rest."* Trust Him. Trust my Son, Jesus.

I am your mother, and I thank you for your response.

19. Our Lady's Request   JULY 24, 1992

Call On Me and My Son

My Child,

If you are to follow my Son, you shall always be challenged, and there are many forms of persecutions. Stand strong in your faith and do not let temptations lead you into doubt. When you are being put to the test, call on me and my Son, and we shall come to your aid.

I would ask that a three day fast of my priest and his people be made in order that the fallen angel does not interfere with my plan in this church of my spouse which is to lead my children to my Son and back to God, their Father. If I do not have the cooperation of my faithful children, then many souls shall be lost. They must pray for their brothers and sisters that are so lost in their sinful ways that they cannot find the light.

It is a special time of graces that are flowing from the Father, but so many of my children are filled with hatred that there is no room for this grace in their hearts.

Do not judge those that condemn my visits. Merely pray for them, for they know not what they do! I am their mother, too, and it saddens my heart that I am met with such consternation and condemnation, but I continue to pray for them and hope that my messages will be accepted and that I shall receive acknowledgment for them.

I am your mother, and I thank you for your response.

20. Our Lady's Request   JULY 26, 1992

There Are Many Messengers

My Child,

Do not be disturbed by the utterances of men. You should not be concerned if your actions please men, but that they please God.

You shall see me by my Son—on the Cross—to the left, but I shall also reveal myself to others and reach others in different ways and in different places on this eve of September 1, at the midnight hour.

Do not be anxious, for I am with you and shall protect you.

Tell all that my messages have not changed and to listen to my messengers (for there are many at this time). Listen to my messages, and **live them**.

I am your mother. Thank you for your response.

[*Visionary's Special Note:* I was somewhat in an anxious state and was afraid that the news media might discover my identity in some way. I knew that this would possibly detract from the importance of Our Lady's appearance at St. Joseph Church and was so concerned about it that I was even considering not going to the church that night. As I prayed about it, the message above was her answer. Thank you, Holy Mother for always being there for me.]

21. Our Lady's Request   JULY 30, 1992

Look Beyond What You See

Be at peace. Look beyond what your physical eyes are beholding, and you will see a greater plan at work here, for all that is happening now has a reason, and it is my intention so that I may reach many of my children and in order that my messages be sent out to all of my lost children.

Know that it is through these efforts of so many that some of those who have strayed shall return to the right path and come home again to my call.

I am your mother and ever with you. Thank you for responding to my call.

[*Visionary's Special Note:* The above message came to me after I was somewhat distraught over all the attention of the news media and other people concerning Our Lady's promised visit at St. Joseph Church on August 31, 1992, at midnight. This is Our Lady's way, she never leaves you alone to struggle through your inner conflicts. She is also appearing to me and the other lady every day in order to strengthen our faith and to encourage us to trust her. She appears to each of us separately—and wherever we may be. This other lady and I are also in close contact and are strength for each other. I have no doubt that Our Lady will keep her word and that she will definitely appear there, but I am troubled about all the negative things some people are saying about her.]

22. Our Lady's Request   AUG. 3, 1992

Realize You Are a Child of God

My Children,

So many of you are entwined in the world of the physical that you have lost sight of who you truly are. You are a child of God, and you are neglecting you soul. You are feeding the desires of your bodies but are starving your souls.

Why are you hoarding your physical treasures? They will surely pass away. Many of you live your lives as if you were meant to be on earth forever. Oh, my dear children, don't you understand that you are meant to live with God forever?

Make peace with your lives and convert them, turn them around. If you do not convert [or change] your ways now, then it will be too late and you will condemn yourself to live forever, not with your heavenly Father, but with the fallen angel.

I, your mother, plead with my Son on your behalf, so that you will not be lost, but the choice must be yours.

I am your mother, and I have come to call each one of you. Thank you for your response.

23. Our Lady's Request   AUG. 4, 1992

Give Your Life Back to God

My Child,

If the people do not like or do not want to hear the message, they will always attack the messenger.

It is my desire to extend my hand to all of my children on earth. I am doing this with my messages and by way of my children who have chosen to aid me.

In all of the earthly confusion, do not lose sight of the goal, which is to lead mankind back to God. So many think they can live as they please and sometime later in their life, they will reconcile with their Maker. But I tell you that time is short, and the trumpet is prepared to blow.

Man has always been given free choice, but in a foolish and unwise act, they have abandoned God. Even now many have come to deny the existence of God. My child, if you deny the existence of your own Father, how could you come into being? How could you explain your birth or your creation? Denying God will not make Him go away. God does truly exist and is **real**, as all of you are real, and He is always watching over you.

Many of you, my dear children, have made a total shamble of your life. Decide now to give your life back to God and let Him work miracles for you. He is delighted to give you His gifts, but, in turn, you must be willing to accept them in order to receive them.

My visits to you are one of His gifts. I will continue to be with you and help you, but if mankind refuses to open their hearts to me then I shall be called home again. My children, I long to draw you close and lead you to my Son and your Saviour. Why do you refuse to follow?

I am your mother and I thank you for your response.

24. Our Lady's Request   AUG. 11, 1992

The Mt. Adams Steps

[*Visionary Note:* When I questioned Our Lady about why she had chosen to appear in this area the following was her answer to me:]

My child, I have come to this area because of the faith I find here and because I find many sincere hearts here that are united to my Son, Jesus.

I have witnessed the trials of my people here and also witnessed their desire to follow my Son, Jesus.

The faithful souls who walked the Way of the Cross with my Son to my church on the hill has found favor with the

Father, and my visit to your area is a special grace bestowed on you at this time.

I am your mother, and I am pleased at my children's response.

25. Our Lady's Request   AUG. 11, 1992

I Have Come to Your Land in a Special Way

My Child,

I have come to your land in a special way as there is a special need here for all of my children. The Prince of Darkness has targeted the youth of America to help him to defeat my mission here.

As Our Lady of Light, I shall call the children back to God and show them the way. My light shall overshadow the darkness, and with the help of my faithful children, we shall together defeat the plan of Satan to claim the souls that belong to God.

Pray, pray, pray, my children, that you, too, do not fall into the hands of the Prince of Darkness. I, your mother, shall protect you and cover you with my own mantle, but first, you must choose to do God's will.

If you do not choose to convert your lives, then I am helpless to lead you on the path of salvation.

I am your mother, and I thank you for your response.

26. Our Lady's Request   AUG. 13, 1992

Put Jesus in the Midst of Your Life

My Dear Children,

You must convert your lives and live it out only for God.

Dear Children, if my Son, Jesus, came into the midst of your daily life, would you run and hide or would you welcome Him there.

I am here to tell you that Jesus is in the midst of your daily life, even if you cannot see him.

I am your mother and thank you for your response.

27. Our Lady's Request   AUG. 14, 1992

Pray for Peace

My Dear Children,

Today I call you to prayer especially for **peace**.
You should not wait to pray until wars begin, but pray
and fast *before* they begin.
By prayer and fasting, wars can be stopped.
I am your mother, and I thank you for your response.

28. Our Lady's Request   AUG. 15, 1992

Forgive Your Brothers and Sisters

My Dear Children,

I am blessing you today with my motherly blessing. Today
many graces shall flow from the Father.
Be at peace, dear children, so that you might know these
graces.
I ask that you forgive your brothers and sisters and carry
no false witness against one another.
Love one another so that the peace of God may enter your
lives.
I am your mother, and I thank you for your response.

29. Our Lady's Request   AUG. 17, 1992

Learn To Choose Wisely

Dear Children,

Learn to choose wisely. It is not God who causes wars,
but man who brings this action on himself by the choices
he makes of his own free will.
Until you choose to live in peace with your brothers and
sisters, there will always be wars. Dear children, peace must
start with you, each in his own heart. Make peace with your
neighbors and make peace with your God.
Forgive one another. We are all one family and with God,
Our Father, there is no division. You can all claim the
inheritance of Heaven, and you do this by choosing peace.
I urge you to pray with your heart so that peace can be

yours.

I am your mother and thank you for your response.

30. Our Lady's Request   AUG. 18, 1992

If You Do Not Believe, You Cannot Hear Him

Dear Children,

You must **believe** or you will not receive. If you do not believe in God, then you are closed and cannot hear Him.

My children, *believe* for then you will hear God speaking to your heart and hear His words.

If you lose your faith, you could lose your soul. My children, I urge you to restore your faith and to begin today to lead a holy life.

If you wait until tomorrow, it may be too late.

I have come to call you to come home to your God.

I am your mother and thank you for your response.

31. Our Lady's Request   AUG. 20, 1992

You Are A Miracle Yourself

Dear Children,

Where is your faith?

You are seeking miracles everywhere. My children, don't you know that you are a **miracle** yourself.

Inside a tiny acorn is a glorious tree. And inside each of you is an even greater miracle.

Each of you have been given this gift of your life by God the Father.

How many of you have ever thanked Him?

I am your mother and thank you for your response.

32. Our Lady's Request AUG. 31, 1992

[*Editor's Note:* The following message was given by Our Lady in July with instructions that these requests be given out on August 31, 1992. Crowd estimates that day ranged from six to eight thousand.]

I'm Calling You Back To My Son

My Dear Children,

Thank you for responding to my call. Your presence here is a sign of your faith to me.

To those of you who see me, this is God's gift. To those of you who don't, believe as if you do. For I am here among you. I am **real**!

I have come to renew your faith and to walk with you in your trials of these times. So many of you have locked God out of your lives. You should know that this is the reason for the chaos you now have on earth.

I come to you today to ask for your help. Yes, I need you my children, to accomplish my plan for peace.

It is my desire that you choose now, this day, to lead a holy life and to be a good example to others.

I desire that you reclaim moral values and put the salvation of your spirit above the desires of your body.

I desire that abuse and violence be halted in order that the innocent, especially the children do not have to suffer for it.

I desire that those of you who have full cupboards share with those who have nothing.

I desire that each of you do your part to bring peace into your own community and your family. Encourage family and community prayers.

My children, do not worship false gods by placing your money and material things before the Father. Do not look to others to change their ways, but examine yourself. Do not just listen to my messages, but share them especially with my other children who do not know me, for I have come for all my children, and I am calling them all to God's graces.

My time with you is short and you must act now before it is too late. Remember, dear children, there is no sin you could have that God will not forgive. Trust in Jesus' Mercy. He has sent me, His Mother and your Mother, to tell you this.

I am your mother, and I love you. Come home, my dear dear children, to my waiting arms. I want to take you to my Son, Jesus.

I thank you for this reponse.

Chapter IV

A Spectacular Occurrence

Visionary's Report of Aug. 31 Event AUG. 31, 1992

God So Loved the Earth, He Sent Us His Son.
Jesus So Loved the Earth, He Sent Us His Mother!

On Monday evening, August 31, 1992, along with my family members and close friends, I arrived at St. Joseph Church in Cold Spring, Kentucky. Our Lady had predicted this event when I saw her at the Notre Dame Marian Conference on May 10. At that time, she had requested that I approach Fr. Smith of this parish and tell him (along with other messages) that she would appear at St. Joseph Church at midnight on August 31, as Our Lady of Light, and wished us to honor her as such on September 1, this being the day she first appeared to five of us ladies in a field, one year ago.

Our Lady had previously told me that she would reach many people, in many different ways and in many different places on this night, as a sign that all might believe.

Of course, I had no doubt that she would be there, but I wasn't exactly sure how or to whom she would appear.

Anyway, she did all that she foretold, plus so much more. Just to witness it was such a great blessing, not only for me, but for all who were present, both inside the church and outside. And thousands of people were present.

As soon as we arrived at the parking lot, someone nearby pointed to the sky and said, "Look at the rainbow." It was a small rainbow, but visible to everyone there. I humbly thanked the Holy Mother and prepared to wait to go into the church. Then people started exclaiming, "Look at the sun; it's spinning!" Yes, no doubt about it, something wonderful was in the air already.

Soon afterward, we made our way into the church. I must mention at this time that our Blessed Mother had already told me and the other lady who also sees her that we should look for her by her Son—to the left of the cross—and that is exactly where she was.

As we were all praying the Rosary, she suddenly appeared there. She was turned toward the cross and was bowed down to her Son. Then she spread her arms out and said, "My Jesus, behold my children."

She also knelt at the side of the cross and prayed the Chaplet of Mercy with all of us. She was kneeling and had her hands folded in prayer.

When the people in the church sang the song "Our Lady of Light" they all stood in honor of Our Lady. It was then that I saw Our Lady turn toward the crowd, smiling and spreading her hands out to them, sending them her special motherly blessing.

At one time, the other lady and I both saw her Immaculate Heart exposed and she said *"I am opening my heart to all of my children."*

Our Lady then appeared with three children kneeling in front of her and there was a lamb lying there at her feet. (Our feeling was that this represented Fatima.) Then while we were praying the Rosary, she again turned sideways facing the crucifix and said, *"My Jesus, behold the faith of your children."* I felt such love inside, I felt I would burst. How beautiful she was. Our Lady had done just what she said she had come to do. She took us all to her Son, Jesus.

It was also during the praying of the Rosary that I saw Jesus on the cross looking down at his Holy Mother, and then raising His head and looking at the crowd, He said:

"In so honoring My mother, you have also honored Me!"

Once again, as it always is when Our Lady appears, time seemed to stop, and although I was aware of everything going on around me, I felt I was still somehow removed or distant from it. It is hard to describe.

This time, Our Lady did not come to life in the beautiful statue, but another statue of her was in the area, and at times she seemed to merge with it. She had on a white gown and was wearing a light blue mantle over it. The sash on her waist seemed to be gold. She was in a glimmering and pulsating golden light.

When the sound system went off, and Fr. Smith knelt waiting patiently for someone to fix it, Our Lady just looked down at him smiling. Then I saw a golden light flash from her heart to Father Smith, and it covered him. She told me this was the love for him, her son, and she was placing him in her protective shield. I remember wondering if he possibly felt this. It was all so very beautiful.

There were mysterious flashes going on in the church earlier, and they continued throughout the evening. These were much like flash bulbs or streaks of lightning. In fact, the security people in the Church kept sweeping the crowds with their eyes to see if someone was taking pictures. Cameras were not permitted in the church; anyone entering the church had to leave their cameras outside. So just where were all these "flashing lights" coming from? Where, indeed!

I knew, as well as the people accompanying me, exactly where they were coming from and from whom. You see, whenever Our Lady appears to any of us, these flashes of light are always nearby. So, we knew when they started that she was there.

Our Lady had told me that this light was God's grace. So, I'm sure that is what was taking place here—God's grace was showered on the people there and also throughout the church itself. The people outside of the church filling the parking lot and surrounding area also were blessed with these mysterious flashes of light which were witnessed by the thousands that were there.

Near midnight, Father Smith was leading the Rosary for the people both inside and outside of the church (loud speakers were set up in the area outside the church) when suddenly there were very brilliant streaks of golden light sparkling around the front of the church and over the altar area. It was then that Our Lady became much brighter and looked directly at Father Smith. It was then that Father Smith stopped praying and after a moment of silence said, "Let us pause here for a moment and welcome Our Lady in our midst.''

Again, I wondered if he was aware of her presence or felt her looking at him. As we continued to pray the Rosary, Our Lady looked over the crowd of people and seemed very pleased.

When they started the Benediction service, Our Lady was holding an open book in her hands. I was not told what the book was but came later to realize that it was ''The Book of Revelation.'' She also held something in her right hand that appeared to be a long rolled-up scroll or scrolls of some kind. I feel that these had something to do with the book she was holding. My lady friend and I both saw this at exactly the same time because we were telling each other what we were seeing and it was identical.

It was during the Benediction service that the statue of St. Joseph near the altar seemed to become real. He had a gold chalice in his right hand and tilted it forward so that we could see there was red liquid in it. My friend and I both saw this, too, and both felt that St. Joseph had brought the Blood of Christ to add to the Eucharistic Host on the altar. So, the Body and Blood of Christ was then present on the altar. St. Joseph also held out his staff to the crowd of people in the church at different times and seemed to be blessing them with it.

During the Benediction, Our Lady had turned to face the crucifix on the altar again and knelt with her head bowed. After the service, she turned to the people again and turned her head as she looked over the crowd, smiling all the while. Only once did I see her look directly toward the area where we were sitting and smile lovingly at us. One of the gentlemen with us also said he saw her turn her head back and forth. Apparently, he witnessed her looking at the people there.

When the other priests came on the altar for the Benediction service, they didn't realize that Our Lady was present directly behind them. She smiled down at them and reached her hands down toward them and sent them her blessing. Here, too, I wondered if any of them felt this or perhaps felt her gaze upon them.

It was near midnight that we also noticed from inside

the church, that all kinds of lights were flashing from somewhere outside the church. If I didn't know better, I would have thought there were ambulances, fire engines, or police cars outside with their lights all flashing—that's how prevalent the lights were.

While inside the church, all colors of lights were flashing everywhere—from the high ceiling to the floor. The lights seemed to go through solid objects and even the people. I don't know if the other people present were aware of this or not. Later, when I questioned the others, they said they had also witnessed this flashing of lights on the altar.

There were five in our group who saw Our Lady that night. Two of us saw basically the same thing, but one lady with us said that when she saw Our Lady turn to face the Crucifix, she seemed to be pregnant, and she thought this was odd. How beautiful. Perhaps this also ties in with the "The Book of Revelations" as it states that the woman with the twelve stars around her head would be with child.

I am just giving my own personal feeling and interpretation here of what we were witnessing; it is for others who are more qualified to examine these visions taking place. As for me, I did not observe her being pregnant.

My niece told us that she observed Our Lady turning toward the outside wall and seemed to bend down and go through the wall. I wonder if this was when the people outside the church said they observed her figure in light on the church wall? I'm sure that walls would be no barrier for Our Lady.

One of the other ladies said she thought she saw Our Lady raise her arms up. That must have been when she was sending her motherly blessing to the crowd.

My aunt said she saw a lot of colored lights flashing around the statue of St. Joseph on the altar. I wonder if this was when that statue became real?

So, you see, I, like you, have a lot of questions myself but of one thing I am sure; Our Lady certainly fulfilled her promise to appear at this church, St. Joseph (the church of her spouse) in Cold Spring, Kentucky, and she did just what she said she would. She reached a lot of her children in many different ways and in many different places on this evening.

I, like many of you who were present this blessed evening, have no doubt whatsoever that we all witnessed a great blessing from God—whatever you choose to call it.

Do I believe in miracles? You better believe it! I have been privileged to touch many of them.

I am documenting this event for my own personal benefit and because Our Lady instructed me to keep a written journal of it. I would like to state here, once again, I am not trying to prove anything to anyone else. I'm simply sharing my wonderful experience with anyone who is interested.

I would like to further comment here that I have since this night, heard of many extremely wonderful experiences that took place outside the church on the church grounds by some of the thousands who were present. However, these were not my experiences, so I cannot comment on them further.

I realize that many of you are wondering and asking "Did Our Lady say if she would return here at another time and date?" She has said nothing more to me than to give out her messages which she wanted to be sent far and wide to all of her children in the whole world. These are her messages that are enclosed in this story and the ones that were given out to the people that evening. So this has been done. Now perhaps, the rest is up to us.

As to why she calls herself "Our Lady of Light," she replied, *"Am I not the Mother of the Light?"* She further stated, *"I have come as Our Lady of Light to spread my light into your darkened world. My messages have not changed. They are the same. As at Fatima, so it is today. I was with you then, and I am still with you today."*

Fr. Smith in Medjugorje vestment, a gift of the Gospa prayer group

Grotto of Our Lady of Lourdes, Immaculata Church, Mt. Adams

Altar and Sanctuary of Mother Of God Church, Covington,
Kentucky. (Note cover photo)

Mass in St. Joseph parking lot the morning of August 31.

Our Lady's Outside Grotto at St. Joseph's

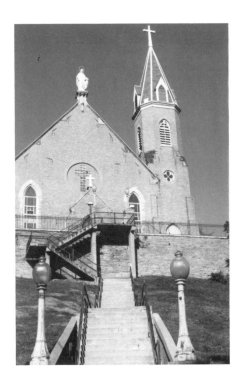

A full view of the steps and front of Immaculata Church, Mt. Adams.

The sign by the side of the church

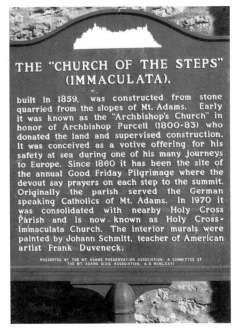

THE "CHURCH OF THE STEPS"
(IMMACULATA),

built in 1859, was constructed from stone quarried from the slopes of Mt. Adams. Early it was known as the "Archbishop's Church" in honor of Archbishop Purcell (1800-83) who donated the land and supervised construction. It was conceived as a votive offering for his safety at sea during one of his many journeys to Europe. Since 1860 it has been the site of the annual Good Friday Pilgrimage where the devout say prayers on each step to the summit. Originally the parish served the German speaking Catholics of Mt. Adams. In 1970 it was consolidated with nearby Holy Cross Parish and is now known as Holy Cross-Immaculata Church. The interior murals were painted by Johann Schmitt, teacher of American artist Frank Duveneck.

PRESENTED BY THE MT. ADAMS PRESERVATION ASSOCIATION, A COMMITTEE OF
THE MT. ADAMS CIVIC ASSOCIATION, A.D. MCMLXXXI

Panorama view of Ohio river and Kentucky shore from
Immaculata Church, Mt. Adams.

35mm photo of grotto taken the night of August 31. Shows
unusual light activity.

"Pieta" in St. Joseph Church

Our Lady of Grace
in St. Joseph Church

Main Altar in
Immaculata Church

Typical light phenomena the night of August 31. Pictures captured from a standard T-120 NTSC video tape by a digital freeze of a frame on a Hitachi color video printer. Pictures taken by home movie camera mounted on a tri-pod. There was no camera motion. Above picture shows tree branches as lighted with church window lighted in unusual manner. Below, the same film shows window area— only the lighted window was over 100 ft. distant from the camera which was in a stationary mode in St. Joseph parking lot aimed at the side window of the church.

Fatima grotto in Immaculata Church

Our Lady of Grace overlooks St. Joseph Church

Chapter V

Ave Maria—
Our Lady's Requests Continue

33. Our Lady's Request SEPT. 3, 1992

To Fr. Smith

My Beloved Son,

Because you have been receptive to my wishes I shall shower down on you and your parish many graces and blessings. The church of my spouse shall become a Haven of Peace for all who are weary. Many who have been lost shall find their way here.

For my light shall remain here and I will continue to grant many favors to those who come to me here. Many shall find me here in many different ways in the days to come.

Know that the seeds you have planted shall grow and many souls will thus blossom in faith because of you, my son.

I hold you ever near to my heart, and I shall carry you through all your trials. Know that at the time of your death, I shall walk with you to the Father.

As you have opened your heart to me, I open my arms to you.

I am your mother and I am grateful for your response and for the response of my children of your parish.

34. Our Lady's Request   SEPT. 4, 1992

Miracles Will Follow

My Child,

I did not say I would send a miracle on August 31 at midnight, but that I would appear there at the Church of my spouse.

The miracle I promised on December 8, 1991, was just that, as the end of Communism was my miracle to the whole world.

I tell you now that my children have given a miracle to me in that so many of them showed me and my Son their faith by gathering in such huge numbers for prayer.

Know that the event I promised has taken place, and now the miracles will follow. Through the grace of the Father, many shall be healed both in body and in spirit.

I shall continue to remain at this holy place and will continue to manifest myself to many of my children any time they seek me out. This is a great gift of the Father. I shall intercede for any of my children who ask. I shall carry their desires to my Son and plead on their behalf for their requests.

Do not become heavy in heart, but rest in the peace of my Son for all that has been accomplished through you for the honor and glory of God, the Father.

I am your mother, and I thank you for opening your heart to my requests. I shall continue also to remain with you, ever close, and ever near.

35. Our Lady's Request   SEPT. 4, 1992

I Shall Remain Here

My Child,

This evening was not only for you on August 31 at midnight, but was for all the others also.

As you know, I had asked you to be there so that you could be present to witness this precious gift of the Father to His people. He has permitted me to come to my children in this special way on this evening. Through His grace, I shall remain and continue to shed my motherly blessing on all who come to this place.

I shall continue to guide you and instruct you. Stay focused on my Son, Jesus.

I am your mother, and I thank you for your receptive response.

36. Our Lady's Request   SEPT. 9, 1992

Open Your Hearts—Pray For This Grace

Dear Children,

God gave you your life to share with Him. Many of you have refused this. My children, if you do not welcome God into your daily life, then He may, likewise, not welcome you into Heaven.

I urge you to convert and embrace the love being offered by your heavenly Father. Open your hearts. Pray for this grace.

I am your mother and thank you for your response.

37. Our Lady's Request   SEPT. 16, 1992

Our Lady of Hope

My child, the rainbow in the sky is God's outward sign to man of His promise and for mankind's hope. Read the Scriptures.

As He has sent me to you as Light to lead you out of the darkness, you might also refer to me as "Our Lady of Hope," for I signify God's rainbow.

I am your mother and thank you for your response.

38. Our Lady's Request   SEPT. 23, 1992

"Behold How the Christians Love One Another"

My Child,

Just as my messages and signs are meant for all, and not only for you, so, too, are they meant for all my children of every faith—not just my children of the Catholic faith.

You should respect each other's faith and share with one another your love of God. In the early days of the Christian Faith, others would remark, "Behold how the Christians love one another."

Could they say this of you today? You should always be a good example so that you may lead others to my Son, Jesus.

I am your mother and thank you for your response.

39. Our Lady's Request   SEPT. 27, 1992

America, The Center of Peace

You do not realize that all in your path are part of my plan. All are an intricate part that is needed to fulfill my plan for peace—especially here in America, which shall become the Center for Peace—and shall spread it worldwide.

I am your mother and thank you for your response.

40. Our Lady's Request   OCT. 22, 1992

A Font "Consecrated to My Immaculate Heart"

My Child,

I do thank all of my children who welcomed me to the church of my spouse. I further desire now that a water font be placed near my resemblance in order to proceed with my plan for this parish.

I ask that this water source be blessed and consecrated to my Immaculate Heart on the eighth day of December.

From this water shall spring forth abundant graces. I, your Mother, shall send forth my motherly blessing to all who honor me here.

I am your mother and thank you for your response to my request.

41. Our Lady's Request   NOV. 25, 1992

Return to the Roots of Your Faith

My Children,

You do not realize the seriousness of my visits to you. My time with you here grows short, and soon you must be able to withstand the tribulations alone without my presence. I am your mother and do not want to see the loss of so many of my precious children.

Choose now to walk with God, for the time is swiftly coming when it may be too late.

Return to the roots of your faith, and practice it. Do not only listen to my messages, but practice them.

You have strayed far but the door of God's grace is open now, and you can be redeemed of your errors. I beg you to come through this door, before it closes. You do not see what chastisements will befall the earth if God's children do not convert their lives, but I assure you, it is **very serious** and many shall suffer the consequences, even the innocent. Pray and fast, dear children, in order to prepare for the days that are coming. Wear blessed objects and keep them in your place of abode to offset the plans of Satan to ensnare you into evil ways.

Forgive, forgive, dear children, so that peace may reign in your world.

Prayers of the heart, and especially the prayers of the innocent children, can bring about the opening of closed hearts, so that they can see the error of their thoughts.

Be ever watchful, dear children. I shall never abandon you. Please do not abandon me.

Listen to my messages and help me to save you.

I am your mother and thank you for your response.

42. Our Lady's Request   DEC. 3, 1992

It Is Never Easy to Follow the Steps of My Son

My Child,

Come to my church on the Hill and I shall lift you up. Concentrate on the passion of my Son as you walk the way of His Cross, and you shall be enlightened.

I will come to you there and shall console you. Be not sorrowful, for I, your mother, am always at your side.

Let not the comments of men sway your faith, for you know what is right.

My child, it is never easy to follow the steps of my Son, but, if you only ask, the grace shall be given you to withstand any pressure.

I am your mother and thank you for your response.

43. Our Lady's Request   DEC. 3, 1992

Fr. Smith, I Have Great Plans
For My "House of Mary"

My Son,

Do not be concerned with the wishes of men. Strive only to please God. I am with you and my mantle shall protect you. Focus only on my light and you will not be led into darkness. Your temptations shall be heavy but I will help you carry your burden. The Holy Spirit shall also sustain you, and console you in your time of doubts. Because you have accepted my wishes, many graces shall be granted unto you from the Father.

Let not your heart be troubled. Your way shall soon become clear. I have great plans for my **house of Mary** of which you are a very important part. I wish that this place also be consecrated to my Immaculate Heart on the first day of May, and that many souls be led to peace here. It should be a haven of rest for all that are weary in whatever way. I will oversee the work done there and my presence shall come there amongst you.

As you have been faithful to me, my dear son, I will strengthen you and lead you into my light. Together we can lead the stray souls back to my Son. Be of happy heart and know that all is transpiring according to my plans.

For all, there is a reason, and it shall become apparent in God's time.

I am your mother and thank you for your devotion.

44. Our Lady's Request   DEC. 3, 1992

Make Peace, Show Love—Not Hatred

Dear Children,

Why do you hold grievances with one another? I wish all of you to make peace with your brothers and sisters, and to behave in the manner of the children of God. I desire you to be good examples to others, show compassion, not contempt. Show love, not hatred. Do not harbor resentment against one another, for when you do, you are pleasing Satan, who is now raging a strong war against my wishes and those of my Son. I urge you to make peace with yourselves and with each other, so that, in harmony, you may walk in my light.

I desire that you make your hearts a pure vessel to receive the Christ-child, whom I am presenting again to each of you.

On the eve of the date (Christmas), I will again come amongst you, if you will open your hearts, and bestow my motherly blessing on all that honor me and my Son. The location of my faithful souls will not matter, for I shall find them. Those who are suffering for the poor souls shall be especially touched, and receive abundant graces.

Look into your own hearts, dear children, and prepare them for the coming of my Son, the Child Jesus.

I am your mother and thank you for your response.

---

45. Our Lady's Request   **DEC. 21, 1992**

Fr. Smith, I Am With You,
Even When Others Abandon You.

My son,

I know the heaviness of thy spirit and the feeling of your abandonment. I shall help you with your burdens and I shall not abandon you. I am with you, even when others desert you.

I and my Son have always been rebuked and scoffed at. Though it saddens my heart when my children turn away from me, I do not love them any less. I ask that you pray for them and show them love.

I will not remain where I am not welcome, but I will reach out to my children at any time they approach me with a humble devotion, regardless of where they may be.

I have given and sent many signs to my children there, but many refuse to accept them and refuse to honor my visits.

My son, you have done all you could do—now, leave the rest to me and **trust me**. I can move mountains and I can melt even the coldest hearts.

Let not your heart be troubled, for in your acceptance of my wishes, many souls have found their way back to their Lord. Without your acceptance, this would not have been possible.

My foundation for peace at the church of my spouse (St. Joseph's) has been laid (on August 31, 1992) and it shall proceed as planned, regardless of the actions of some that oppose me there—so be at rest. However, this unfoldment shall take place in God's time, not man's.

Though your feet carry you in other directions, rest assured that I will accompany you for there is still much to accomplish. My motherly mantle shall protect you.

Pray especially for the persecuted, for there are many. Let love shine forth from you and let forgiveness be your password. I again call your attention to the "Golden Cross." I ask of you a three day fast (of your choice), for my intentions.

I am your mother and thank you for your devotion and for your acceptance to my call.

46. Our Lady's Request   DEC. 21, 1992

Be of Strong Faith

Dear Children,

As Christmas approaches—look into your hearts and cleanse them in order to be a fit dwelling place for the Christ-child.

This is a special time for plenary indulgences and for many graces. **Ask and you shall receive**.

Do not be lax in your faith and guard it with perseverance, for the fallen angel is very strong and is attempting to lure you into false beliefs. He is targeting the youth and especially the leaders in the Father's houses (all churches). For if the buildings fall, the foundations shall rot and crumble.

Be of STRONG FAITH, and do not assume that you cannot be touched by God's chastisements, for they could not see in the country of Yugoslavia what lay in their future and neither can you see what may be coming to your land.

PRAY, dear children, PRAY. I ask that you LOVE ONE ANOTHER.

I am your mother and thank you for your response.

Chapter VI

Jesus Speaks—To All Of His Clergy

DEC. 4, 1991

Pray And Be Pure Apostles

You have enlisted
in My spiritual army,
and in so doing,
have become one of my
apostles.

You do not realize the
great power
that has been bestowed
on you.
Some of you have ignored
or abused this blessing.

Search your souls
and discard any
negativity you find therein.
I need you to be a **pure**
vessel—
As the spiritual **war**
has now manifested into
your physical world.
Pray, that you may not be lost!

89

2. Jesus Speaks—To All Of His Clergy　　　DEC. 4, 1991

Retrieve My Children

As a missionary, you are blessed with such graces, but in searching the fields for the lost sheep, you have overlooked the children in the home.

They have been neglected and have abandoned their souls to evil ways.

Retrieve them and feed all the hungry.

Whatever you do for the least of my brothers, **you do for me!**

3. Jesus Speaks—To All Of His Clergy　　　MAY 21, 1992

The Good Shepherd Is Coming

I am the Good Shepherd, and have come to attend my flock.

So many of my sheep have become lost, and for too long they have been neglected. My priests and all of my clergy are my appointed shepherds in charge of and over the sheep that are mine. These sheep have chosen Me and are so marked by their Baptism or Confirmation and their testimonies.

They have wandered away into the valleys of doubt and denial. **Retrieve them.** Many are caught up in thickets and snares, and their rescue shall be hard. But, I, your Master, shall aid you in this journey.

True, you may get scarred by the thorns and thistles of ridicule and condemnation, but you must trudge on and fulfill your duty, which is to do the work I entrusted in your hands.

I urge you to appoint and designate helpers to help you accomplish this enormous task, for it is of the utmost importance that my lost ones be found and reclaimed.

How do you appoint helpers? Enlist the aid of the sheep still in the herd. If they send forth their calls to return home, the lost sheep may hear them and follow their sound.

The battle is raging, and if they are not welcomed home and saved again, then they may be gobbled up by the wolf, who is close at hand.

The war of good and evil is now taking place, and I, the Good Shepherd, your Lord and Master, have come to your aid. Put your hand in mine, and you shall not falter. I send you My peace; take it to your brethren. You who have the light must let it shine. You cannot sit in your huts and wait for those lost to return. They cannot see you. They cannot hear you. And they will not find you, unless you leave your post temporarily and go out into the wilderness and search them out.

Let the cry go forth that the Good Shepherd is coming and will be reclaiming the sheep that are rightfully His, and His legions are in attendance in both the spiritual realm and in the physical. You must put on your armor of faith and lead the faithful forward.

As the Father has sent Me, I now send you.

Peace be with you.

4. Jesus Speaks—To All Of His Clergy   SEPT. 16, 1992

Go Forth and Evangelize

[*Editor's Note:* There was a discussion relative to Jesus addressing His messages to all of His clergy versus the message of Our Lady addressed specifically to the priests. The following messages from Jesus and Our Lady provide clarifying insight concerning the discussion which occurred at that time.]

It is the will of the Father that all of His ordained ministers, in whatever walk, are instructed and requested to be better spiritual leaders of their congregations. So many of them have gone by the wayside and are even leading the others astray.

I have given these directions by the authority of the Father, for His Divine Will is being ignored throughout all the earth by the leaders of every faith.

I remind you that in the eyes of the Father, all religions are equal. It is man that made the divisions. Just as you should not place one another before each other, so, also, do not place one faith above another. For all of you are God's children, and He loves you all the same with no division.

Therefore, I speak to all of my disciples, all the same, and I do so by the authority of my Father. It is His Divine Will.

I am Jesus, your Lord and Master.

[*Editor's Note:* The phrase "in the eyes of the Father all religions are equal" within the context stated sparked further discussion. Again clarifying messages were later received from both Our Lord and Our Lady.]

SEPT. 24, 1992

Be at peace. The clarity of My words has always brought confusion to the minds of men, even my followers when I was on earth.

I say unto you again that, in the eyes of the Father, all religions are equal in that the Father sees into the purity of their intentions, and has accepted any and all who honor their Creator with this desire of pure intention.

However, many who are under the banner of the different religions have not placed God first in their lives, and unless they convert their ways and return to God the Father, with a pure heart, they will fall from the grace of the Father.

I have said that "you should love your Lord and your God with your whole heart and soul, and you should love your neighbor as yourself." This has not changed. Put the Father first, above all, and then your neighbor. You are all God's children, and you must act as such. Love your God and love one another.

I say to you also that in the future, the time shall come when I again come unto you. I shall call under my roof, all who have served Me. **Through the grace of the Father**, all who have served Him with fervor and had even the smallest desire for redemption, shall come to know Me as the true Son of God and as their Redeemer and Saviour, and then, they, too, shall come under My roof, at which time the wall of division shall crumble and disappear. There shall be then, one fold and One Shepherd—and My Kingdom shall have no end. Peace be unto you.

I am Jesus, your Lord, Master and Redeemer.

SEPT. 24, 1992

[*Editor's Note:* Our Lady of Light also spoke the same day on this matter.]

My Child, on the matter of all religions being "equal,"

I have spoken already to my other messengers concerning this. All men are equal before God and before me, but, of course, not all religions are equal, for there are many who are using the name of God and religion for their own selfish purposes. These souls need prayers, for this is a grave error.

While it is not necessary that you belong to the Catholic Church to be saved, it is certainly necessary that you give respect to God's commandments and follow the dictates of your conscience, for God sees into your soul.

All of you, whatever religion you may have, are created in the image and likeness of God, and will someday come to rejoin the house of the Eternal Father. So, in this phase, all of you are God's children and are equal.

God will extend His grace to everyone, and salvation is available to *all* of you, with no exception.

It is those of you who deliberately refuse and deny God who shall condemn yourselves to Hell.

Dear children, respect each others religions, and do not look with contempt on those in error, but pray that the truth may be revealed to them, through the grace of the heavenly Father.

You do not understand the power of prayer from the heart. These prayers will unleash the grace from the Father, and through His grace, all souls can be saved.

The roots of all religions on earth are placed in the Father, and He, likewise, nourishes all with His unconditional love.

Just as the energy of the sun warms all, with no exception, so, too, does God's love flow into all of these roots. However, there is only one tree—Jesus Christ the Son of God—and although there are many branches, all will eventually blend into the one tree, this being the "One Fold and One Shepherd."

This shall come to pass in God's time, not man's.

I am your mother and thank you for your response.

NOV. 25, 1992

My Child,

You asked for understanding of "in the eyes of the Father."

I tell you again that you are thinking in the terms of man's limitations.

Man cannot perceive anything with the same vision as the Father. Neither can man comprehend that activity of the mind of God with His abundant flow of graces for His own creatures.

All are equal to the Father, because all of you are His children. You are loved, dear children, even when you offend by your sinful behavior. Through the grace of the Father, you are forgiven.

My children, I do not wish you to squabble over who is best and who is most favored before the Father. Do not judge others and do not judge other religions. You must respect each other and respect each other in their choice of worship to the Father.

The Father shall determine the purity in their hearts and in their acts of devotion to Him. Do not be concerned as to the equality of your religion, for the Father shall bring all into balance. Look into your own hearts and into your own intentions, and do not place yourselves first, because in the eyes of the Father, the first may be last and the last may be first.

I am your mother and thank you for your devotion.

5. Jesus Speaks—To All Of His Clergy   SEPT. 16, 1992

When I Shall Come Again

Many are wondering and asking when I shall come again.

I say unto you, no one knows the hour but the Father, but He has sent My Mother to prepare the way, so you would be wise to listen to her.

Always stay in readiness so you are not found asleep.

I am your Lord and Master, Jesus.

[*Editor's Note:* There was a discussion concerning the relevancy of the many apparitions taking place on earth and the Second Coming of Christ. The additional messages of Jesus and Our Lady again provide clarity on a topical matter.]

OCT. 8, 1992

My Child,

As already spoken, only the Father knows as to My Second

Coming when I shall again come unto you in glory, and will gather My sheep, but be ever in readiness so that I do not come upon you as a thief in the night.

I am Jesus, your Shepherd and Redeemer.

OCT. 8, 1992

My Child,

The heavenly Father has given many revelations as to the Second Coming of my Son to reclaim the earth. These are in the Holy Scriptures already written. As foretold, these signs are now upon you and are unfolding. Read the Holy Bible and you will see that only the Father knows the day and the hour. So, be at peace and always stay prepared.

My coming to my children on earth is a gift of the Father and is also foretold in the Holy Scriptures. It is a time of great graces and abundant blessings from your heavenly Father. I have come to bathe your souls in my spiritual light, but many of you refuse to come out of your darkness. I am calling all of you to pray so that your hearts will open and be receptive to God's love. Pray that the cup of chastisement you have drawn on yourselves can be lessened.

Pray and fast, dear children. Pray and fast.

I am your mother and thank you for your response.

Chapter VII

The Hidden Flower

1. Background and Identity

Some unusual correspondence was written in early December 1991. One letter dated the Feast of the Immaculate Conception, allegedly from Our Lady contained a prophesy. It was transmitted by Cyndi Cain, an alleged locutionist. The prophesy and some other messages received by Cyndi Cain constitute this chapter.

Cyndi and Michael live in Bella Vista, Arkansas. Their lives are dedicated to God. As part of their ministry they direct the Mir-A-Call center and publish the bi-monthly newspaper. "A call to peace." Cyndi, the Hidden Flower of the Immaculate Heart, has been receiving daily locutions from Our Lady for over three years. It is Our Lady who has called her the Hidden Flower. She and Mike are under the spiritual direction of Fr. Al Svobodny, O.M.I. They have taken a solemn vow of poverty at Our Lady's request to more effectively communicate Our Lady's messages to her children.

There a degree of risk in publishing a visionary's experiences, especially when there are associated unusualities such as pre-announced appearances and annonymity. To include another in the same book was a difficult decision. Finally, Our Lady was asked for guidance. Her alleged decision then became a matter of belief and obedience.

2. The Prophesy

Extracted verbatim from the letter allegedly from Our Lady, dated December 8, 1991, is the foretelling which follows.

I solemnly tell you, and especially my beloved priest-son Fr. Smith, that he shall bring unto all my children that ineffable sweetness of God's Holy Presence through his devotion to My Immaculate Heart. This place where you have chosen, my dear ones, shall become a place of great devotion, a place where immeasurable graces shall pour forth upon the troubled people who seek consolation from Almighty God. I solemnly tell you that by your faith, your prayers and sacrifices, and your frequent reception of the Sacraments, that I will visit my children in this holy spot, and I will manifest myself to those who come in faith and are humble and little of heart. It shall be a place of great cures and conversions, and there will be many who will come because my children are starving to be fed with the Truth, which is my Divine Son. In so many places around the world, my dear ones, my Divine Son is profaned in the Tabernacle, and no honor is given to me, as the Mother of God, which is not in accordance with God's Holy Will. This place named for my beloved earthly spouse, St. Joseph, who's power before the Throne of God is great and is yet not recognized by the people of God, shall be resplendent. Here, too, I shall gather my little ones who come and shall bestow upon them the conversion of heart that is necessary to abandon oneself completely to God. I desire families to come, from the youngest to the oldest, and there in this abode of grace of Love, to be reconciled one with the other, for the family is the symbol of the Trinity, and is to be renewed upon the face of the earth as the Second Advent approaches rapidly.

In faith do I ask all of you to make a novena to my Immaculate Heart and to the Sacred Heart of my Divine Son, and to make one also to St. Joseph. Call upon St. Joseph especially in times when there seems no way to continue, when you are tired and weary, and you have no human feelings of God's presence within you. He, too, knew what it was to live on total faith, and he surmounted all difficulties through His ardent faith in the Author of all creation. So shall he, who is the protector of the family, protect and help to make of you one holy family united in love through my Immaculate Heart, that all the world may witness the presence and power of God and give unto Him the glory and praise that is due to Him.

In this holy place I wish to renew the devotion to the Eucharist, which is so sadly lacking, and which in many places has become an abomination before the Throne of the Trinity. I ask my beloved priest-son, Fr. Smith, to assist all my children to renew in themselves interiorly and exteriorly the practice of worthily receiving the Body and Blood of my Divine Son, and to practice such reverence in His August Presence, that you will understand that where He is, so is the entire Heavenly Court and all the angels bow down in worship, and I am there with my Son, worshiping Him who is the Saviour of the World.

Meditate and ponder well my words, my dear children. It is God's Holy Desire to make of you His humble servants, and I will speak words to my children who come and will bestow God's peace and graces upon those who, through the Will of God, shall receive them in faith and bear witness to my presence among you.

Do not be afraid of those who speak against you. Do not be anxious over any who offer opposition. Bring all things, no matter how small, to me, and I will give you the answer you need and guide your every footstep in the way of Light and Truth, for I am the Queen of Peace, the Mother of God and the Mother of all my children everywhere. Let the word be spread far and wide, and bring my little ones to me. Yes, as you have already said in your chapel, they do not need to touch me. Rather, by God's power and love, and through the love which emanates from My Immaculate Heart in union with the Sacred Heart of My Son, I shall touch them.

AUG. 29, 1992

3. Outside Indianapolis Enroute to Cold Spring

From Cyndi Cain's Journal

Beloved Hidden Flower, I am with you. Am I not a mother whose maternal care is constant? Have I not promised you that I would take care of you until you are in Heaven? Therefore, be at peace, for you walk the path that God wills for you.

I solemnly tell you that I come to all of my children as a path of light. This light is God's Truth, and all who seek Him must know the Truth. Therefore, by His authority, I come, a light for my little ones, a pathway which leads unfailingly to my Divine Son.

My children have not understood how intense is the spiritual darkness of these last days. They cast their eyes about for a visible darkness, which shall come, but remain blinded to the very real darkness which covers their soul.

My children have been lulled into a false sense of security in this time of false peace. Each of my little ones not gathered beneath my Mantle contributes to this veil of darkness because they refuse to be open to God's sublime graces.

Therefore, I come, Mother of God, bearer of light, to be among you as a shining beacon in this very urgent time. Come to me, your Heavenly Mother, and permit the Light to engulf you, enlighten you, inflame you. I wish to call all of my children home, to bestow upon them my Son's peace, and to heal their wounded hearts. All who seek my Son, all who believe in simple, childlike faith shall know that I am with you in this extraordinary way, lighting your way to the Sacred Heart of my Son. Heed my words, which are given you in love.

Pray! Fast! Wait and watch. I am the Bridge of Light. Thank you for responding to my call!

AUG. 30, 1992

4. St. Joseph Church, Cold Spring

From Cyndi Cain's Journal

From the seven hills I call all my children. From the seven hills I will gather all my children. Come, and be not afraid. Come, and no longer doubt. I, the Mother of God, will light the way of my Divine Son. Am I not your Mother? Come, come home for I call with an urgent plea.

During Communion

My child, beloved of My Mother's Immaculate Heart, I ask you to tell all that I give to them My Mother. I do not desire doubt and ridicule, for I, your God, sent her to be with you.

I will not allow the darkness to deepen. I sent

her to Light my Path. And I solemnly tell you that
he who holds My Shepherd's staff in this place
shall embrace the light I so generously give.

AUG. 30, 1992

5. Immaculata Church, Mt. Adams (overlooking Greater Cincinnati)

From Cyndi Cain's Journal

Beloved Hidden Flower, behold, I, the Mother of God,
have come to this area for the sufferings and sacrifices, the
labors of the holy souls who bore good fruit in their earthly
journey here have made a pathway of love to reach to Heaven.
I come upon this pathway. I come by God's Authority to
renew that which has grown muddied by sin. Here in this
place, where once great honor was given to my Divine Son,
I now find that He is mocked, scoffed at. His very Presence
is denied. Thus, I come, and there will be the fire of God
within many hearts. A new and bright light is coming. A
beacon, a torch by which I will find my lost children. I
will establish here a pure refuge of heavenly light that all
might once again believe and return to the embrace of God.
Here in this place will come many miracles. Many shall
manifest the power and mercy of God. Here I ask all of my
little ones by means of their faith, their trust and their love,
to renew the pathway of light which has grown dark. Behold,
I am here, the Mother of God. Behold, I prepare the way
for my Son!"

6. A Message through the Anonymous Visionary

[*Editor's Note:* This is Our Lady's response to the visionary concerning a request for guidance about Cynci Cain's
messages being included in this book.]

SEPT. 27, 1992

My Child, it is my desire and my request that Cyndi Cain's
messages be included in my movement as Our Lady of Light,
but here, too, she must accept to share them, as they per-
tain to my visit at the church of my spouse.

She is much beloved of God and should be reminded that
through suffering, you are moved closer to the heart of God.

It is my wish that the witness of my signs to her be used as testimony to the fact of my real presence at the church of my spouse—as well as my church on the hill.

I am your mother and thank you for your response.

AUG. 30, 1992

7. The Complete Renewal of Religious Life

Beloved Hidden Flower, I am here with you. Do you not see me? I solemnly tell you that the faith of my little ones which has been shown here will not go without its reward. Therefore, I have come. And it is my desire that from this area there will come the complete renewal of religious life throughout the world, starting with the monastic life. It is from this area that I will give the graces for the renewal of the religious life, and from here that this renewal will spread to all the country, and from there to the world. Do not be concerned, nor doubt, for the ways of God are infinite, and His power is without limit. Pray and fast! Make this part of your daily life. Know that I, the Mother of God, have truly come as Our Lady of Light, and I will speak to many hearts. They shall hear me and know that I have come to gather my children back into the Light, which is my Divine Son. Pray! Pray! Pray! I need all prayers, which I gather as bouquets to lay at the feet of my Son. Time is most critical. Come home to your heavenly Father, my children, while there is yet time. I love and bless you. Thank you for responding to my call!

Chapter VIII

Commentary

1. The Issue of Creditability

Although a task for future properly qualified authorities, some discussion is appropriate. Our Lady mentions in her September 4, 1992, request that she did not promise a miracle on the eve of August 31. In reviewing some sixty-five written testimonies submitted to the pastor, one finds an array of experiences. These include claimed visions and sensations of the nearness of Our Lady, the ability to look at the sun and experience its dazzling effects, rosary chains turning gold in color, conversion of hearts especially those of skeptical attendees, many receiving the sacrament of confession, and other such things including unexplainable light phenomena witnessed by thousands. This same kind of light activity, incidentally, was documented at Fatima in 1917.

The light phenomena and the other things experienced by those at St. Joseph's on August 31, and also experienced on a frequent basis by the visionaries and their friends, may be considered as signs. Do they point to the balance of the September 4 message? *". . . and now miracles will follow. Through the grace of the Father, many shall be healed both in body and in spirit."* The words of the original prophesy that St. Joseph Church would be a place of great cures and conversions also come to mind.

Our Lady has said: *". . . and the unfoldment of my messages will be the proof."* Therein to a great extent shall the issue of creditability be determined. She also stresses *"God's time"* and *"all will unfold as planned."* Pressing the issue of creditability for a conclusion *now* is senseless. The matter of promised miracles is her responsibility, as is ultimately the whole issue of creditability. Be patient. Rest easy. Endure.

The ultimate factor concerning creditability is always the fruits, the souls yielding to God as a result of this prodigy. This issue becomes quite large when one begins examining the message content. We may fuss and stew and become immersed in discernment without realizing that this issue is not all that difficult for Our Lady. She does not have our barriers and boundaries. An extract from a private message makes this point very explicit. *"Tell him the creditability he seeks is mine to deliver, as I shall prove to all that I have truly come here to St. Joseph Church as 'Our Lady of Light' with the events and miracles that shall unfold in the days to come."* Creditability is hers. It may come about by properly authoritative decree or by leaving the children of the Church full liberty to form their own judgment. In any event, it will be difficult to disclaim creditability if and when the unfolding occurs, and likewise one cannot claim creditability with sureness when the message implies the proof shall unfold in the days to come.

2. The Fatima Message Has Not Changed

If the reader wishes to relate this book to something that we are familiar with, go back and browse through Our Lady's request number ten, entitled "My Message Has Not Changed."

In this request she reminds us that she came at the beginning of this century to aid us, and she pleads her cause again in great detail and does so emphatically. She asks us to open our hearts to her, and that she will then show us the way to save ourselves, to convert our lives back to God, and to be responsible for the free will given us. She again tells us to use the same effective tools she advised at Fatima seventy-five years ago. She armed us then with the Rosary and the Scapular and told us to pray unceasingly and start fasting. She says, *"My message has not changed and I am delivering it once more.''* These are truly the pleading words of our Blessed Mother.

The following statements extracted verbatim from a personal message, and previously mentioned following Our Lady's request number four to substantiate a different position, is repeated here to emphasize the sameness of her cause.

OCT. 26, 1992

My Child, I pointed out to you that in Fatima during the early part of this century, I also came as "Our Lady of Light," and the reference to the "New Era" had already begun even then. All of my appearances, then and since then, are connected together, for I am the same Lady, and my messages are the same. As at Fatima, so it is now. You are thinking in man's time, not God's. Be patient, for all shall unfold on schedule, but in God's time.

It is interesting to note that at Fatima Our Lady was likewise referred to as Our Lady of Light. The Bruce Publishing Company of Milwaukee published a book, *Our Lady of Light* in 1947. This book, a scholarly work, was first published by a Portuguese Jesuit, Gonzaga da Fonseca, professor at the Biblical Institute in Rome. It was adopted in a French translation by Canon Chanoine C. Barthas which received high commendation. Joseph Husslein, S.J., Ph.D. of St. Louis University, was the General Editor of the English translation with imprimatur. It was copyrighted and published by Bruce. Though now out of print, it is in the Xavier University and Thomas More College libraries in the greater Cincinnati area. Nine pages of this book discuss the atmospheric prodigies associated with the Fatima apparitions. When you read this book, the similarities with the Cold Spring events are striking.

3. They Speak of Chastisement

It seems that all of the seers—and at this time there are many—bring to the fore the subject of chastisement. Let's try to understand this notion in an overall sense, and particularly as it relates to the messages herein. In a broad perspective, a chastisement, or warning thereof, is a punishing or censuring act to discipline, correct or purify. When Our

Lady speaks thusly, she does so in the sense that everything foretold can be changed, lessened or eliminated by the intervention of our prayers, our conversion to God and our reparative penance. Our Lady speaks frequently in this manner. These words are spoken in the sense of chastening or corrective warnings. Let us look at several of her messages to better understand this idea in the particular context of this book. This is repetitious and redundant, however, it is also a good way of focusing on a particular subject.

1. 10/28/91—To the People of America—*If you continue to turn away and insult your Maker, you will draw serious consequences upon you and your land. . . . I am asking you to change your lives and convert before it is too late. . . . Do it now, for tommorow may be too late. The time on the clock grows shorter.*

5. 2/9/92—The Catholic Church Should be the Catalyst— *It is the time of fulfillment of many Scriptures, as well as the unfoldment of my messages to my children on earth through the Fatima messages.* (Note also that Jacinta, the little Fatima seer who died shortly afterward spoke from her hospital bed: "If men repented of their sins, Our Lord would forgive them; but if they do not change their lives, the chastisement will come.")*. . . I urge all of you to continue to pray my Rosary and to urge all of your brothers and sisters to do so also. In this way, I can continue to intervene and forestall, if not eliminate, the catastrophic events to befall earth as a chastisement for their errors.*

12. 6/16/92—Focus on my Son—*I have told you the cup of chastisement is now flowing on earth and it shall touch all of you, the good and the bad, before it evaporates.*

In the broader context of this subject look also at Mary's role in her coming to us now. She states it in many ways, for instance: *"I have come to lead my children back to their spiritual paths and back to God. . . "* Keep in mind also these words from the fifth message of Jesus: *"No one knows the hour but the Father, but He has sent my mother to prepare the way, so you would be wise to listen to her."* Simply stated, she has come to earth with the authority of God the Father and with a specific task to accomplish. Should one not believe then that God will accomplish His purpose and that the force of His chastisements will depend upon our responsiveness to His emissary? The ways of any chastisement or Second Coming will be by prayer and suffering. We have a choice to make. Look at the purifying process man must yet go through to correct just one item, the outrageous, accursed evil of abortion. This taking of life from the womb is both a direct rejection of God's act of human creation and an undermining of the entirety of Christian life. How will we come to this total realization when many of society's other values and attitudes are similarily decadent? Are we asking this question with a sense of despair instead of joyful hope? The alternative to the chastising hammer of God's bountiful mercy and justice is the great plan of Our Lady. We may be vastly underestimating the power of our prayers and sacrifices and her reparative actions, powers and messages.

Our Blessed Mother does not have our boundaries, our barriers or our limits, but she does have the authority and power of the Triune God.

Our task then is to focus on the positive aspects of her counsel. It is easy to visualize a great struggle between the forces of good and evil in the immediacy of future events. It is a blessing to be able to so discern. But our job, our responsibility, is positive, responsive action. We must begin by opening our hearts to her motherly pleadings. She states it so simply in her beautiful sixth request: *"Give me your hearts and I shall transform them for you."* We can do nothing about chastisements per se, but we can respond with ardent love and veneration to the call of the mother of Jesus. Just desire it, and it will happen. She is here, ever so near.

The preceeding words address to the subject of chastisement in a brief broad sense and in a little depth concerning some of the chastising messages herein. As this subject is so topical in Marian circles at this time it seems appropriate to go just a bit deeper. St. Alphonsus Maria de Liguori, Doctor of the Church, 1696-1731, wrote nine separate discourses for the times of calamities. Each of these discourses comprise several pages of manuscript and are published in volume eighteen, "Miscellaneous Subjects," of his Complete Ascetical Works. Though many years out of print they should be available in most Catholic University libraries. The titles of these Discourses describe their content and are listed here to give the reader further insight into this subject.

Nine Discourses for Times of Calamities

1. God threatens to chastise us in order to deliver us from chastisement.
2. Sinners will not believe in the Divine threats until the chastisement has come upon them.
3. God is merciful for a season, and then chastises.
4. The four principal gates of Hell.
5. External devotions are useless if we do not cleanse our souls from sin.
6. God chastises us in this life for our good, not for our destruction.
7. God chastises us in this life, only that He may show us mercy in the next.
8. Prayers appease God, and avert from us the chastisement we deserve, provided we purpose to amend.
9. Most Holy Mary is the mediatrix of sinners.

4. All Mothers Are Called

A nice lady I know was asked a question as to why Jesus and Mary so often choose women to appear to and communicate with. Her general response was that women are creatures of love and understand and respond more readily to a message of love. This may not be the best explanation, but have you ever noticed the preponderance of women at the shrines of Our Lady and the leadership roles they fill in the Marian centers and prayer activities? Our Lady fully understands and she is very specifically calling out to all mothers now to help her. It is more than a pleading; it is an exalting call to join her great spiritual armada. Her successive requests, numbers seven and eight, are very clear and specific: *"Your children are at stake. Your families that are so torn apart must be restored to the throne of dignity."*

Mothers of America, can you do it? Oh, how powerful you are! It is not a question of "can," it is a statement of "will." Open your hearts to her love so you may be filled with the Holy Spirit and she will join you and lead you in all of your prayers and actions.

In her twenty fifth request she states that the Prince of Darkness has targeted the youth of America to help him defeat her mission here. Oh mothers of America, please hear her call. Join her great joyous work and turn this tide of decadent morality in our country. Please respond. We need you desperately!

5. "Our Lady of Light" Has Come to This Area

We have seen that Our Lady has chosen America to become the Center for Peace and to spread this peace worldwide. What a truly great gift this is for God to give our generation of Americans. You are now asked to consider your many personal blessings and then to ponder the amazing graces to be bestowed in this area of our wonderful country as you consider these exerpts from her requests.

> ". . . *Look beyond what your physical eyes are beholding and you will see a greater plan at work here . . .*"

> "*I have come to this area because of the faith I find here and because I find many sincere hearts here that are united to my Son, Jesus.*"

> "*I have witnessed the trials of my people here and also witnessed their desire to follow my Son, Jesus.*"

> "*The faithful souls that walked the Way of the Cross with my Son to my church on the hill (Immaculata Church) has found favor with the Father, and my visit to your area is a special grace bestowed on you at this time.*"

> ". . . *From this area will come the complete renewal of religious life . . . and from here this renewal will spread to all the country, and from there to the world.*"

"...I will establish here a pure refuge of heavenly light...here in this place will come many miracles, many shall manifest the power and mercy of God..."

"...And now the miracles will follow....I shall continue to remain in this holy place (St. Joseph Church)...I shall continue to remain with you, ever close and ever near...many shall find me here in many different ways in the days to come."

"The Church of my spouse shall become a Haven for Peace for all who are weary. Many shall find their way here who have been lost."

"...I ask that this water source (St. Joseph) be blessed and consecrated to my Immaculate Heart on the eighth day of December.
From this water shall spring forth abundant graces. I, your Mother, shall send forth my motherly blessing to all who honor me here."

In reviewing this matter of Our Lady's intentions for this area, we wondered what her desires were for the ongoing rehabilitation project of the old nearby St. Mary's Seminary and former archbishop's residence which is being converted to a Marian activity center. Her answer was not long in coming.

"As for the Seminary project he refers to—this shall all be accomplished through the grace of God. I have many plans here but will need the consent of many of my children to make them blossom, for I must honor their free choice. Many prayers are needed here by my faithful children as the devil does not want to see my plan here go into action. I shall guide them and defend them, but I also need the help of my children. You must pray and fast, dear children, pray and fast, for the time is so short, and the need is great. Do not lose faith, and do not become lukewarm. Many of the curious have already abandoned their pledges to me. This saddens my heart and the heart of my Son, Jesus."

It almost takes your breath away to grasp the significance of Our Lady's words. Wow! Can this really be true? Is it believable? Should one test the spirits? Yes, of course. But Our Lady goes further than that. She acknowledges she is appearing to many at this time and in many different places, and she gives us a guarantee. *"In the discernment of these appearances, you shall know the truth by the forthcoming fruits of each event. The truth shall be revealed in the bearing of the fruit."*

Remember also, the words of Father Abraham to the rich man who had asked him to send the beggar Lazarus to warn his five brothers: *"If they do not listen to Moses and the prophets, they will not be convinced even if one should rise from the dead."*

You may be assured that her presence here (especially at St. Joseph and Immaculata Churches and Marian Center being formed at the old St. Mary's Seminary) is a significant part of God's plan for the triumph of the Immaculate Heart of the Mother of God, which is to lead to the reign of the Sacred Heart of her Son. Our Lady has given Her word. It is a pledge. She will prove to all that she has truly come to us here at St. Joseph Church as Our Lady of Light with the events and the miracles that shall unfold in the days to come.

How truly wonderful the prospects are in Mary's great plan for this area. But she needs our responsive prayers and good works. Let each of us pledge our prayers and our actions to further her cause so that the tri-state area may be so significantly graced with her many plans.

6. The Role of Our Lady

Looking briefly at some of the statements herein help define the role Our Lady has given us in these messages and the foretold desires and events we are to yet witness.

"I say unto you, no one knows the hour but the Father, but He has sent My mother to prepare the way, so you would be wise to listen to her."

"The grace of the Father has permitted me to be with you . . ."

"My coming to my children on earth is a gift of the Father and is also foretold in the Holy Scriptures."

". . . I ask you to tell all that I give to them my Mother. I do not desire doubt and ridicule, for I, your God, sent her to be with you."

"I send her to light my path."

"Behold, I am here, the Mother of God. Behold, I prepare the way for my Son!"

The word "precursor" would seem to summarize Our Lady's role. Her statements are consistent with the text of Vatican Council II: "For all the saving influences of the Blessed Virgin on men originate not from some inner necessity, but from the divine pleasure."

To proceed further in this mode of thought then consider:

". . . I have come through the Catholic Church because these are my only children that recognize me and accept me, but even many here also refuse my extended hand."

". . . I remind all that I am the Mother of all and have come to aid all of you in your trials and sufferings."

And so she also comes to all of her children as their mother. And again we continue:

"I, as the Queen of this light, have come to many of you either directly or indirectly, and asked for your allegiance and your help in bringing about my plan of peace for your earth, which I am also a part of."

"I desire that the Catholic Church should be the catalyst to unite all faithful souls under one roof."

Thusly, she comes as precursor and as the mother of all. She also brings with her a plan of peace for our earth, and in that plan is the task of the Catholic Church to be a catalyst in the divine process of uniting all faithful souls under one roof.

On page 189 in the book In *Our Lady of Light,* previously referenced, is this sentence: "His Eminence, Cardinal Cerejeira, has proclaimed that a new era is opening upon the world, that of the Immaculate Heart of Mary." His Eminence was D. Manual Goncalves Cerejeira, the Cardinal Patriarch of Lisbon, Portugal. How prophetic were his words. Please note again the extract from the October 26, 1992 personal message. *"My child, I pointed out to you that in Fatima during the early part of this century, I also came as 'Our Lady of Light,' and the reference to the 'New Era' had already begun even then."*

The "New Era" is a term not yet specifically defined. But we do know that Our Lady has come to prepare the way for her Son. Everyone is also quite aware that only the Father knows the timing of this event. The messages here of Jesus, vigilant as always, are very clear on that point. His messages are to the clergy of all faiths and they stress the urgency and magnitude of the tasks to be accomplished but they do not even alude to the immediacy of His second coming. What is clearly stated is that Our Lady is here with us with the full authority of the Father and that we would be wise to listen to her. God is not capricious. His statements are consistent with Scriptures. The difficulty is the acceptance of the timing, its physical nearness, and the alluded scope of the events to come.

We have seen that Mary's plan started even at Fatima. Part of it is now unfolding here and has been for some months. In trying to determine what is ahead of us here and elsewhere we have little idea. However we do have some startling messages. Consider those having to do with the scriptures. But also consider concurrently the changing times from Fatima to today. This sense of the times is captured in a one sentence quotation, again from the "Our Lady of Light" book: "The very word 'Sin' is almost forgotten on the lips of men and its very notion clouded; morality has hardly any other rule than free caprice, personal interest or pleasure."

Contrast that second quarter of our century observation to a fourth quarter heavenly perspective of Our Lady from *Calling All Mothers: "Look around you. The whole world is in utter chaos."* One might assume that Our Lady's request to open Scriptures to record the great manifestations of the handiwork of the Almighty relates to our mad rush of immorality. This message of opening Scriptures has enormous implications. It appears that a great moment or moments in the world's history are soon to arrive. Man has a searching mind and a vivid imagination, but the only hint of foretold reality is the ageless warning of vigiliance.

We do not know if the request to open Scriptures signifies change that only the perspective of history can grasp correctly or whether it is a request to record a tumultuous tide of events. We assume, though, that it is to be epoch in significance. We have been told there will be continuing revelations and ongoing experiences and both private and public appearances. By her words, our actions and inactions are preparing a bitter cup, and if we do not respond to her messages and convert our lives we will have to drink it. The cup of chastisement is flowing and it shall touch all before it evaporates. The time is short that she has left with us. If we consecrate ourselves and all of our families to her Immaculate Heart and to the Sacred Heart of her Son, Jesus, we will have protection from the evils of the world. We will be wise to listen to her. As the rainbow in the sky is God's outward sign to man of His promise and for man's hope, she comes also as Our Lady of hope, for she signifies God's "rainbow."

7. I Am Jesus, Your Lord, Master and Redeemer

The messages of Jesus are all addressed to the clergy of all faiths. This fact was questioned and clarity assured. He speaks at the will of the Father to *all* of the Father's ordained ministers, in whatever walk of Faith. Stop for a moment and consider this singular fact. Jesus is speaking at the direction of God the Father to all of God's ministers. He speaks to them broadly of equality and respect and their need to place God first and above all. He instructs them to be better spiritual leaders and for many to convert their ways. He speaks of the purity of intentions and the compassionate mercy of the Father's acceptance of the desire of pure intention. He speaks of coming again and that He will be accepted as the true Son of God and as our Redeemer and Saviour. He also says that those who fail to convert and return to

God with a pure heart will fall from the grace of the Father. The words of Jesus and the clarifying comments of His Mother are a summation and overview of all that has been said.

The call to all of God's clergy is clearly to go forward and evangelize the world. His basic precept has not changed. Put the Father first, above all, and then your neighbor. Love your God and love one another. This is not just a message or book for Catholics. Jesus is speaking to everyone and Our Lady comes as the mother of all. There are no exceptions. None.

The clergy of all religions need to recognize the great strength of unity and place emphasis on commonality of purpose rather than points of division. We must pray that those who know with clarity the faults and failures of mankind will speak out in their own faith, and yet as one, to re-awaken God in the minds of all people.

Jesus's call is a command to action. He recognizes the task is enormous. His advice to His clergy is to appoint and designate helpers. The phraseology He uses is biblical but very clear. The war of good and evil is ongoing and His disciples are to get out of their huts and to lead the faithful into battle. They are not to wait for his coming, as souls are at stake. He will bring all under one tent when he arrives, but the task of re-establishing morality in the world is ours to accomplish. He has entrusted His mother, chosen by the Father and spouse of His Spirit, she who brought the Light into the world to lead us in this redemptive phase. Her force is enormous. All the powers and grace of Heaven are at her command. Her faithful children on earth are responsive to her call. God makes no mistakes. He chose rightly. She will achieve victory.

The words of Jesus bring great hope. His statement that the Father sees into the purity of our intentions, and has *accepted* any and all that honor their creator with the "desire" of pure intention is a magnanimous proclamation of mercy and love and to humanity a great fountain of relief and of hope. What great comfort it will be to the discouraged and depressed.

Jesus also recognized that his words bring confusion to the finiteness of our minds. Many questions are raised in his messages. But his mother brings much understanding in her words; "Dear Children, respect each others religions and do not look with contempt on those in error—but pray that the truth may be revealed to them, through the grace of the heavenly Father.

You do not understand the power of prayer from the heart. These prayers will unleash the grace from the Father, and through His grace, all souls can be saved."

When we live and pray from our hearts, our loving desire is heard by God and by our souls. He sees into our hearts and the truth of our intentions. If we follow His commandments, the true dictates of our conscience and pray from the heart, we will by our example evangelize the world. When we change, those around us must react to accommodate the change they see in us. It's that simple. Prayer from the heart is the mysterious key that sets it all in motion. It is little wonder then that Our Lady's message is always pray, pray, pray.

Dearest Mother Mary, may all of your children hear the call of your Immaculate Heart and come to rest in the comfort of the Sacred Heart of your Divine Son.

8. Epilogue

We can analyze, acclaim or criticize what has been written. This accomplishes little. We cannot change the past or determine the future. We can, though, open our hearts to God. We can choose from this book that which we perceive as good and from God.

Singularly we can recall these things to memory, and beg God to help us incorporate them into our lives as virtues. When such decisions are present we can thus surrender and align our will to His. We can even make this an offering to honor the life and passion of her Son.

Our Lady has told the visionary that the chastisements she speaks of will be revealed to some as such, but that others will not recognize them as chastisements. Will this not often be because their minds and their hearts are preoccupied or closed to God? She has also revealed that each one, in his or her own heart, will know when they are being chastised for the Holy Spirit shall reveal this to them. We cannot quantify or qualify, but we do know there will be chastisements. Our Lady's last message pointed out that the fallen angel has targeted the youth and the leaders of all churches. Are not these chastisements ongoing? She further said not to assume that we cannot be touched by God's chastisements, for they could not see in the country of Yugoslavia what lay in their future, **and neither can we see what may be coming in our land.**

Our Lady has further stated: *"Soon a time will come when each one shall undergo a personal and individual view into their own soul, and they will see their weaknesses and their falsehoods. Every soul shall undergo this—with no exceptions. Then they will have a choice."* This prophesy is similar to the 1965 reputed warning to the young visionaries of Garabandal, Spain.

Chastisements and warnings are not our Lady's purpose or that of this book. They are alternatives. Is this then our choice; God's light or His Merciful Justice?

Our Lady counsels: Place God first, carry hope, not fear. We must listen to our Lady. Let us not be the author of our own chastisement. Let us rather make prayer a cornerstone of our life, and as a child when in trouble, choose recourse to Mary, our spiritual mother and our Lady of Light.